MATH FACT
FLUENCY

MATH FACT FLUENCY

60+ Games and Assessment Tools to Support Learning and Retention

 **ascd**
Arlington, VA USA

 NATIONAL COUNCIL OF TEACHERS OF MATHEMATICS
Reston, VA USA

JENNIFER BAY-WILLIAMS and GINA KLING

2800 Shirlington Rd., Suite 1001 • Arlington, VA 22206 USA
Phone: 800-933-2723 or 703-578-9600 • Fax: 703-575-5400
Website: www.ascd.org • E-mail: member@ascd.org
Author guidelines: www.ascd.org/write

1906 Association Drive,
Reston, VA 20191-1502
Phone: 800-235-7566
Website: www.nctm.org
E-mail: publications@nctm.org

Deborah S. Delisle, *Executive Director;* Stefani Roth, *Publisher;* Genny Ostertag, *Director, Content Acquisitions;* Allison Scott, *Acquisitions Editor;* Julie Houtz, *Director, Book Editing & Production;* Liz Wegner, *Editor;* Judi Connelly, *Associate Art Director;* Masie Chong, *Graphic Designer;* Valerie Younkin, *Production Designer;* Mike Kalyan, *Director, Production Services;* Shajuan Martin, *E-Publishing Specialist;* Kelly Marshall, *Senior Production Specialist*

Published simultaneously by ASCD and the National Council of Teachers of Mathematics.

All web links in this book are correct as of the publication date below but may have become inactive or otherwise modified since that time. If you notice a deactivated or changed link, please e-mail books@ascd.org with the words "Link Update" in the subject line. In your message, please specify the web link, the book title, and the page number on which the link appears.

PAPERBACK ISBN: 978-1-4166-2699-2   ASCD product #118014   n1/19
PDF E-BOOK ISBN: 978-1-4166-2722-7
NCTM Stock #15799

Quantity discounts are available: e-mail programteam@ascd.org or call 800-933-2723, ext. 5773, or 703-575-5773. For desk copies, go to www.ascd.org/deskcopy.

Library of Congress Cataloging-in-Publication Data
Names: Bay-Williams, Jennifer M., author. | Kling, Gina, author.
Title: Math fact fluency : 60+ games and assessment tools to support learning and retention / Jennifer Bay-Williams, Gina Kling.
Description: Alexandria, VA : ASCD, [2019] | Includes bibliographical references and index.
Identifiers: LCCN 2018033940 (print) | LCCN 2018038568 (ebook) | ISBN 9781416627227 (PDF) | ISBN 9781416626992 (pbk.)
Subjects: LCSH: Mathematics--Study and teaching (Elementary) | Games in mathematics education.
Classification: LCC QA135.6 (ebook) | LCC QA135.6 .B39425 2019 (print) | DDC 372.7/044--dc23
LC record available at https://lccn.loc.gov/2018033940

28 27 26 25 24 23 22   2 3 4 5 6 7 8 9 10 11 12

MATH FACT FLUENCY

Preface

Basic facts truly are *the* foundation on which all mathematical computation is based (larger numbers, rational numbers, operations with variables, and so on). However, too many students leave elementary school lacking fluency with the basic facts. Clearly, the historical (and still prominent) approach to teaching basic facts has been ineffective. This is because there are two fundamental flaws in this type of instruction: (1) a lack of attention to strategies, falsely assuming students can go straight from counting (or skip counting) to just knowing the facts; and (2) a lack of effective assessment, falsely assuming that timed tests can provide meaningful data on student mastery of basic facts. Despite the ineffective and potentially damaging effect of these teaching and assessment approaches, basic fact instruction has changed very little over the years. It is time for a change!

This book is structured around five fundamentals for transforming basic fact instruction. These fundamentals are firmly grounded in research and collectively outline a plan for students that results in lasting learning of the facts, without damaging side effects. By exploring the meaning of numbers and operations, describing their thinking, making sense of the strategies of their peers, and engaging in meaningful practice, students eventually reach mastery of the basic facts, all the while becoming empowered to think and act like mathematicians. Chapter 1 provides a brief, clear description of the five fundamentals. Chapters 2 and 3 describe the learning progressions for addition and subtraction facts, including a plethora of strategies, activities, and games, while Chapters 4 and 5 do the same for multiplication and division. The 40+ games in this book (listed at the end of this preface) are *fun*, but that is not why we included them. Games provide the opportunity to talk about strategies, practice a newly learned strategy, and become more efficient at using strategies until automaticity with the basic facts has been attained. Did you notice how many times the word *strategy* was used in the last sentence? It is that important! This word is often used in many different ways in the classroom, but in this book we only use this term to refer to *thinking* strategies. As you will learn, these thinking strategies are the key to helping students developing lasting fact mastery.

The activities and games featured in this book also serve a secondary purpose: assessment. While students are busy playing games and talking about their thinking, you have an opportunity to employ assessment techniques that will provide far better data than a timed quiz, all the while avoiding the negative impacts of such assessments. Chapters 6 and 7 provide ideas for observation tools, easy interviews, formal interviews, journal prompts, and ways to monitor student progress toward mastery of the foundational fact sets (Chapter 6) and derived fact sets (Chapter 7).

One particular challenge with the basic facts is understanding the myriad of terms: fluency, automaticity, rote memorization, knowing from memory, mental strategies, and mastery. In this book, we focus on the accepted, research-based definition of fluency, which delineates four components: "skill in carrying out procedures flexibly, accurately, efficiently, and appropriately" (National Research Council, 2001, p. 116). This definition expands the focus of mastering facts to include strategies and flexibility, as compared to a focus solely on accuracy and efficiency. Many people, including parents, principals, teachers, politicians, and students, think of fluency as simply being able to say a fact quickly (automaticity). Educating everyone about this more comprehensive notion of fluency is absolutely essential to helping every child learn basic math facts *for life* and feel confident and competent about their ability to do math. Chapter 8 focuses on ways to engage families and other stakeholders in understanding the importance of *fluency*, as well as how they can help their own children become fluent with the basic facts.

Our own advocacy for change, through countless presentations and several journal articles, has resulted in many schools adopting different approaches to teaching basic facts, implementing ideas that are now in this book. These instructional programs and assessment tools have resulted in dramatic change in some schools: more students achieving mastery through games and other activities (as opposed to drill or rote memorization), students becoming more excited about mathematics and confident in their abilities, and teachers feeling that they are doing a better job at preparing their students with the basics. For example, a 2nd grade teacher recently emailed Jennifer this message at the end of the year: "I was a very math-averse teacher who had no idea how to teach students concretely about math. That changed this year with our focus on explaining reasoning strategies and showing their thinking using a variety of visual models. One of the best compliments I got from a student this year was 'I love math.'" Teachers at these sites have often asked us, "Will you write a book?" As we pondered undertaking such a task for several years, we realized that a worthwhile book must not only provide explanations but must also be bursting with activities, games, and tools that could be lifted right out of the book and put to use. That is what we have written. We recognize we are asking for fundamental changes to teaching basic facts. We encourage you to reflect on the way in which our five fundamentals align with your school's basic fact plan and consider how a shift toward incorporating these ideas could affect the learning and experiences of your students. As you identify a focus and a plan, we hope this book will provide you with the activities, games, and tools to support your own basic fact teaching and assessment transformation.

FIGURE P.1	Games in This Book	
Game	**Chapter**	**Targeted Facts**
Game 1: Sleeping Bears	2	Sums within 5
Game 2: Bears Race to 10	2	+0, 1, 2
Game 3: Bears Race to 0	2	−0, 1, 2
Game 4: Bears Race to Escape	2	+/− 0, 1, 2
Game 5: Doubles Match-Up	2	Doubles (sums)
Game 6: Doubles Bingo	2	Doubles (sums)
Game 7: 10 Sleeping Bears	2	Combinations of 10
Game 8: Go Fish for 10s	2	Combinations of 10
Game 9: Erase	2	Combinations of 10

FIGURE P.1 **Games in This Book—**(*continued*)		
Game	**Chapter**	**Targeted Facts**
Game 10: Square Deal	2	10 + __ facts
Game 11: Lucky 13	3	Sums within 20 (and differences from 13)
Game 12: Sum War	3	Sums within 20
Game 13: Bingo	3	Sums within 20
Game 14: Concentration	3	Sums within 20
Game 15: Dominoes	3	Sums within 20
Game 16: Four in a Row	3	Sums within 20
Game 17: Old Mascot (Old Maid)	3	Sums within 20
Game 18: Diffy Dozen	3	Differences within 12 (comparison)
Game 19: Salute	3	Sums and differences within 20
Game 20: Target Difference	3	Differences within 20
Game 21: Subtraction Stacks	3	Differences of 5 or less
Game 22: Around the House	3	Sums and differences that equal 10 or less
Game 23: Dirty Dozen	3	Sums and differences within 12
Game 24: First to 20	3	Sums and differences within 20
Game 25: Sticker Book Patterns	4	Comparing multiplication representations (groups and arrays)

Game	Chapter	Targeted Facts
Game 26: On the Double	4	2s (doubles) facts
Game 27: Trios	4	5s facts
Game 28: Capture 5 First	4	2s, 5s, 10s facts
Game 29: How Low Can You Go?	4	0s, 1s facts
Game 30: Squares Bingo	4	Squares
Game 31: Multiplication Pathways	4	Foundational multiplication facts
Game 32: Fixed Factor War	5	Doubling
Game 33: Strive to Derive	5	Adding/subtracting a group
Game 34: Crossed Wires	5	Break apart
Game 35: Rectangle Fit	5	Break apart, commutativity
Game 36: The Factor Game	5	Division (finding factors)
Game 37: The Right Price	5	Close-by division facts
Game 38: Multiplication Salute	5	Multiplication and division facts
Game 39: The Product Game	5	Multiplication and division facts
Game 40: Net Zero	5	All four operations
Game 41: Softball Hits	5	All four operations
Game 42: Three Dice Take	5	All four operations

FIGURE P.2 Assessment Tools in This Book	
Title	**Chapter**
Tool 1: Observation Tools for Foundational Fact Sets	6
Tool 2: Observation Tool for +/− 0, 1, 2	6
Tool 3: Observation Tool for × 2s, 10s, and 5s	6
Tool 4: Observation Tools for Combinations of 10 and Doubles	6
Tool 5: Observation Tool for × 5s Facts	6
Tool 6: Two-Prompt Interview Protocol	6
Tool 7: Interview Record for Combinations of 10	6
Tool 8: Interview Record for Multiplication Squares	6
Tool 9: Mastery of Foundational Facts Records	6
Tool 10: Rubrics for Foundational Fact Fluency	6
Tool 11: Journal Writing Prompts for Doubles	6
Tool 12: Foundational Facts Progress Chart for Multiplication	6
Tool 13: Observation Tool for the Making 10 Strategy	7
Tool 14: Observation Tool for Any Multiplication Derived Fact Strategy	7
Tool 15: Observation Tools for Selection of Strategies	7
Tool 16: Observation Tool for Strategies and Mastery for Addition Facts	7

Title	Chapter
Tool 17: Observation Tool for Strategies and Mastery for Multiplication Facts	7
Tool 18: Interview Prompts for Assessing Fluency During Game Play	7
Tool 19: Four Facts Protocol Follow-Up Interview Questions	7
Tool 20: Student Records for Addition	7
Tool 21: Student Records for Multiplication	7
Tool 22: Exit Interview for Addition Facts	7
Tool 23: Holistic Rubric for Basic Fact Fluency	7
Tool 24: A Dozen Writing Prompts for Basic Fact Fluency	7
Tool 25: Progress Monitoring Tool for Addition Facts	7
Tool 26: Progress Monitoring Tool for Multiplication Facts	7

Most, if not all, of the 42 games and 26 assessment tools can be readily adapted to other fact sets and operations (e.g., addition games can be turned from sums into products). So, there are truly more than 100 possible games and tools for you—enough to ensure your students are able to truly develop math fact fluency!

1

The Five Fundamentals

You've probably heard it a thousand times: Kids need to be fluent with basic math facts. You've probably seen the word *fluency* on progress reports, in elementary mathematics standards, and in textbooks, but what does fluency actually mean? For nearly a decade, we've been asking this question to teachers and administrators. Common responses include

- "They just know the facts."
- "They are fast and accurate."
- "They understand what the fact means."
- "They have strategies to figure out the facts."
- "It's like when you are fluent in a language—you don't have to think or hesitate much."
- "They are automatic with the facts."
- "They can apply their understanding of the facts to new situations."

As you can see, the school community has struggled to embrace a common and comprehensive definition of fluency. Some definitions focus on speed, while others focus on understanding. Reaching the goal of basic fact fluency requires establishing a shared and complete understanding of the term. As baseball great Yogi Berra once noted, "If you don't know where you're going, you'll end up someplace else." This is the tenet behind the first of our five basic fact fundamentals; the four that follow lay out essential elements for designing an effective plan—one that will help every student learn (and remember) the basic facts while building mathematical confidence and number sense.

Fundamental 1: Mastery Must Focus on Fluency

Procedural fluency includes accuracy, efficiency, flexibility, and appropriate strategy selection (National Research Council, 2001). Note that this definition of procedural fluency applies to all operations, not just basic facts, and these elements of fluency are interrelated (Bay-Williams & Stokes Levine, 2017) as illustrated by the diagram in Figure 1.1.

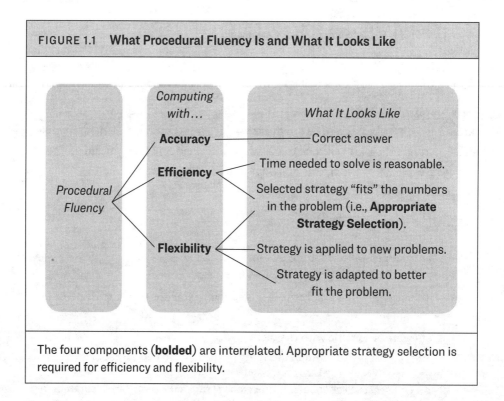

FIGURE 1.1   **What Procedural Fluency Is and What It Looks Like**

The four components (**bolded**) are interrelated. Appropriate strategy selection is required for efficiency and flexibility.

Applying strategies is different than applying algorithms. According to the Council of Chief State School Officers (CCSSO) and National Governors Association (NGA), computation strategies are "purposeful manipulations that may be chosen for specific problems," while algorithms are a "set of predefined steps applicable to a class of problems" (CCSSO & NGA, 2010, p. 85). When students only learn a single procedure, regardless of how quickly and accurately they can implement it, they are denied the opportunity to develop procedural fluency. Strategy selection, adaptation, and transference are critical to both procedural fluency and mathematical proficiency and must be a significant part of students' experiences with the operations right from the beginning, with learning basic facts.

We use these general definitions of each component to focus specifically on basic fact fluency:

- *Accuracy:* the ability to produce mathematically precise answers
- *Efficiency:* the ability to produce answers relatively quickly and easily
- *Appropriate strategy use:* the ability to select and apply a strategy that is appropriate for solving the given problem efficiently
- *Flexibility:* the ability to think about a problem in more than one way and to adapt or adjust thinking if necessary

Consider these aspects of fluency in terms of level of cognition. Which of these requires higher-level thinking? Selecting a strategy, key to both efficiency and flexibility, requires first understanding how and when each strategy is appropriate, and then analyzing a problem to select a viable strategy. Notice that fluency requires understanding, applying, analyzing, and comparing—all higher-level thinking processes. The more students are asked to think at a higher level, the more they learn.

Basic facts are also described in terms of fluency in state and national standards, such as in these examples from the Common Core State Standards (CCSSO & NGA, 2010) (emphasis added):

1.OA.6 (Grade 1): Add and subtract within 20, *demonstrating fluency* for addition and subtraction within 10. *Use strategies* such as counting on; making ten (e.g., 8 + 6 = 8 + 2 + 4 = 10 + 4 = 14); decomposing a number leading to a ten (e.g., 13 − 4 = 13 − 3 − 1 = 10 − 1 = 9); using the relationship between addition and subtraction (e.g., knowing that 8 + 4 = 12, one knows 12 − 8 = 4); and creating equivalent but easier or known sums (e.g., adding 6 + 7 by creating the known equivalent 6 + 6 + 1 = 12 + 1 = 13). (p. 15)

2.OA.2 (Grade 2): *Fluently* add and subtract within 20 *using mental strategies* [with a reference to 1.0A.C.6]. By end of Grade 2, *know from memory* all sums of two one-digit numbers. (p. 19)

3.OA.7 (Grade 3): *Fluently* multiply and divide within 100, *using strategies* such as the relationship between multiplication and division (e.g., knowing that 8 × 5 = 40, one knows 40 ÷ 5 = 8) or properties of operations. By the end of Grade 3, *know from memory* all products of two one-digit numbers. (p. 23)

These standards acknowledge that it is through the application of strategies that a student develops fluency, and it is through the use of strategies that students come to know their basic facts, or develop *automaticity* (more on this point in the next section). However, the activities and assessments traditionally associated with learning basic facts (such as drill, flash cards, and timed testing) exclusively focus on students' accuracy and one part of efficiency (speed), neglecting strategy development. Many studies over many years have compared traditional basic fact instruction (i.e., drill) to strategy-focused instruction. All of them show that strategy groups outperform their peers on using strategies *and* on automaticity and accuracy (Baroody, Purpura, Eiland, Reid, & Paliwal, 2016; Brendefur, Strother, Thiede, & Appleton, 2015; Locuniak & Jordan, 2008; Purpura, Baroody, Eiland, & Reid, 2016; Thornton, 1978, 1990; Tournaki, 2003). We *know* that strategy development is absolutely necessary for fluency. And fluency is essential to developing automaticity with basic facts.

Fundamental 2: Fluency Develops in Three Phases

As students come to know basic facts in any operation, they progress through three phases (Baroody, 2006):

- **Phase 1: Counting** (counts with objects or mentally)
- **Phase 2: Deriving** (uses reasoning strategies based on known facts)
- **Phase 3: Mastery** (efficiently produces answers)

Consider these phases in the context of mastering addition facts. Most students enter kindergarten or 1st grade using counting to solve addition or subtraction problems. They may be counting with objects, on their fingers, or in their heads, but, regardless, these students are still considered to be at Phase 1. As they start to learn some of the easier facts (usually 2 + 2 = 4, 3 + 3 = 6, and 5 + 5 = 10), they can begin using those facts to help them to figure out more difficult, related facts. For example, to find 5 + 7, a student might begin with 5 + 5 = 10 and add on two more to determine that 5 + 7 = 12. This is an example of Phase 2 thinking, where the answer to a more challenging fact is being derived by using a known fact. The flexibility, increased efficiency, and selection of appropriate strategies that are developed in this phase are critical to fluency.

As students engage in sufficient meaningful practice in Phase 2, they become faster in their strategy selection and application and come to know some facts without needing to apply a strategy. Thus, they move naturally into Phase 3 (mastery), which is characterized by the highly efficient production of answers, either through quick strategy application or through recall. Students operating at Phase 3 are considered *automatic* with those facts, as they meet the definition commonly accepted for automaticity—answering within three seconds, either through recall or automatic strategy application (Van de Walle, Karp, & Bay-Williams, 2019). Thus, the difference between Phase 2 and Phase 3 is essentially speed; in both cases, students may be applying appropriate strategies flexibly, but students at Phase 3 answer instinctively within a few seconds, whereas Phase 2 students might take longer to select and apply a strategy.

You've likely seen advertisements for books or fact-learning programs that promise "fact fluency in two minutes a day" or "know your facts in seven days." The reality is there are no shortcuts to developing fluency or to mastery and automaticity. "Quick fix" programs attempt to take students who are operating at Phase 1 (counting) and push them directly to Phase 3, usually through drill and timed testing, skipping any effort to explicitly teach strategies or focus on number relationships. Students subjected to such programs may appear to know the facts in the short term, but within weeks or months they are back to where they started: counting. Because little to no time is spent in Phase 2, once facts are forgotten, students have no efficient, appropriate, and flexible strategies to fall back on. This explains why we sometimes see middle grade students counting to solve basic facts, much to the chagrin of their teachers. In contrast, to encourage lasting mastery of basic facts, students need to have sufficient time and experiences in Phase 2. The activities, games, and assessment tools you will find in this book are designed to do just that.

Fundamental 3: Foundational Facts Must Precede Derived Facts

Perhaps you have memories of learning groups of multiplication facts in order. You memorized the 0s facts, passed a test (and perhaps got a sticker on your chart), and then moved on to the 1s, 2s, 3s, and so on. Although once common, this sequence is not consistent with what research suggests is the most effective approach to learning facts. There are sets of facts within both addition and multiplication that are easier for students to master first and are essential to applying derived fact strategies. We refer to these facts as *foundational fact sets*, or *foundational facts* for short. A foundational fact set is a set of facts that illustrate a specific pattern or number relationship. For example, working on the *one less* facts can be connected to the counting sequence (the number that comes before), to the number line (the number that is one to the left), and to the idea of taking away one.

The remaining facts can be derived from the foundational facts through strategy application. Thus, these sets of facts are called *derived facts*, and students come to know these facts by learning *derived fact strategies*. Notice that we do not use the term *subset* with derived facts. That is because many derived facts can be reasonably solved using more than one derived fact strategy. In fact, students must have many opportunities to select which of the derived fact strategies they will use to solve a combination that they do not know. A flexible learning progression demonstrating the relationships between facts for addition is presented in Figure 1.2. Many studies have found that mathematics teaching based on learning progressions leads to positive effects on children's early math achievement (Frye et al., 2013).

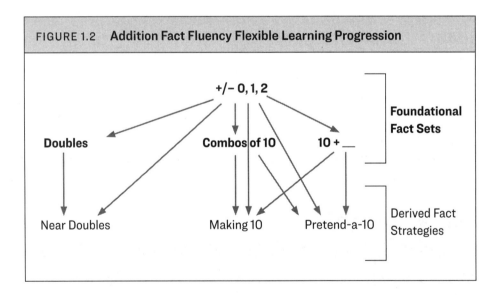

FIGURE 1.2   Addition Fact Fluency Flexible Learning Progression

In this chart we include the +/– 0, 1, and 2 facts as foundational and the place to begin. Notice that each of the other foundational facts, except perhaps doubles, can flow easily from already knowing +/– 0, 1, and 2. Therefore, to work toward mastery of all facts, a first step is to develop automaticity with the +/– 0, 1, and 2 facts. At the next level are more foundational facts, which can be taught in a flexible order, as mastery of one is not needed to reach mastery of another. However, students must master specified foundational facts to use the related derived fact strategies on the final level (e.g., Doubles must precede Near Doubles).

Similarly, multiplication facts can be taught in groupings so that known foundational facts can be used to derive other facts. The flexible learning progression for multiplication is shown in Figure 1.3.

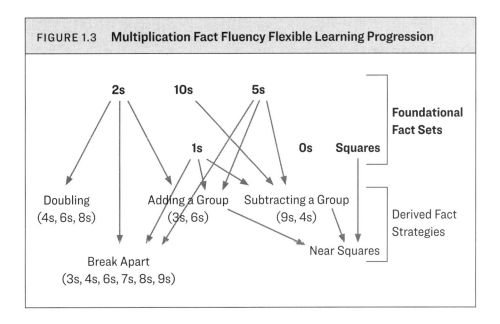

FIGURE 1.3   **Multiplication Fact Fluency Flexible Learning Progression**

The distinction between foundational fact sets and derived fact strategies is essential for effective teaching of the basic facts because it provides a blueprint for monitoring fact instruction progress. Consider the example of finding 5 + 7. If a student didn't already know that 5 + 5 = 10, he would not be able to arrive at the solution as described: 5 + 5 = 10, 10 + 2 = 12, so 5 + 7 = 12. Thus, when we observe students who are unable to use a strategy for finding this fact, we must determine if they have learned the foundational facts to automaticity. If not, that is where intervention must be focused.

Because this progression is so important to students' success with using strategies to master basic facts, we have organized this book around the two groupings of foundational facts and derived fact strategies. Chapters 2 and 4 focus on teaching the foundational fact sets for addition and multiplication, respectively, and Chapters 3 and 5 do the same for derived fact strategies. Chapters 6 and 7 focus on assessing foundational fact sets and derived fact strategies, respectively. The two flexible learning progressions will appear throughout the book to highlight the fact sets or strategies discussed. Our hope is that these charts will not only help you visualize the progression of fact mastery in a typical classroom but also help you with individual progress monitoring in order to develop plans of action to support students who have not yet mastered all the basic facts.

Fundamental 4: Timed Tests Do Not Assess Fluency

Picture a worksheet containing 100 multiplication facts in random order, which students are asked to complete in five minutes. Perhaps you remember these timed tests from your childhood, or perhaps you still see these in use in classrooms today. Now determine how many of the four components of fluency (flexibility, accuracy, efficiency, and appropriate strategy use) you believe are actually assessed with a timed test. We've posed this task countless times to many groups of teachers and administrators, most of whom have initially thought that, at most, two components are assessed—but which two? Flexibility and appropriate strategy use are easily eliminated. Because the teacher only sees a recorded answer, it is impossible to assess if a student is flexible or chooses appropriate strategies from a timed test alone. This does not mean that students aren't flexible or that they don't use appropriate strategies; *the timed test simply doesn't allow a teacher to see it*. What about efficiency and accuracy? Although at first glance it may seem that a timed test can assess these components, there are certainly instances where this isn't true. Consider the following scenarios.

> Tommy is taking his weekly multiplication test. Although he has learned many easier multiplication facts, Tommy still struggles to remember his 7s, and he is very aware of this weakness. Once again, he compensates by skipping around and answering the facts he knows; then he quietly puts his hands under his desk to help him count to answer the remaining, unknown facts. He has learned that he can usually finish the test in time by doing this, and his teacher is therefore convinced he knows his facts.

Ellie feels her heart start to race when her teacher announces it is time to start the weekly addition facts timed test. Even though Ellie excels at reading, writing, and solving even the most challenging story problems, as soon as the timer starts, she draws a blank. She struggles to remember the facts she knows well and is so distracted by the timer that she can't apply her favorite strategies to tougher addition facts, like 7 + 8. With tears in her eyes, she once again turns in an incomplete test and tells her friends she's "just so bad at math." Her teacher is puzzled; she has seen Ellie's automaticity with addition facts many times during math games and doesn't understand why that doesn't translate to the test.

Whether it be from our own childhood experiences or from experiences as an adult, we've all known students like Tommy and Ellie. Let's look at Tommy's fluency. Even though he knew some of the facts, the completed, correct answers on his timed test give the illusion of mastery. The reality is that he is not efficient with all the facts (namely, the 7s), and yet his ability to "play the game" has not only fooled his teacher but also reinforced that he doesn't need to make an effort to learn those facts. Tommy's case illustrates how timed testing does not provide a wide enough lens for evaluating fluency, because it doesn't reveal the exact facts with which students are efficient.

Next, consider Ellie's fluency. She is an excellent mathematical thinker, loves to write and solve problems, and, based on her teacher's observations during game play, has mastered the addition facts. Yet the pressure of time cripples her thinking and essentially invalidates her test as a measure of accuracy. Even worse, this experience has convinced Ellie that she is bad at math when, in fact, she is quite the opposite! Ellie is not unique. In fact, over the past decade there have been numerous findings from psychology and even neuroscience uncovering the damaging effects of timed testing. For example, in a study of more than 50 students in 1st and 2nd grades, Ramirez, Gunderson, Levine, and Beilock (2013) found that students begin experiencing math anxiety as early as 1st grade and that anxiety was not correlated with reading achievement or socioeconomic status. However, they did find an important, troubling correlation: The students who tended to use more sophisticated mathematical strategies were those who often experienced the most negative impact on achievement due to math anxiety. In other words, by age 7, many young students with high mathematical aptitudes are already learning to fear math. Boaler (2012, 2014) also reported that even students who perform well on timed tests share concerns such as "I feel nervous" and "I know my facts, but this just scares me."

Timed testing is often considered synonymous with learning basic facts, and yet, as we have just described, it is highly ineffective at assessing any of the four components of fluency. Why, then, is it still so common? Some schools feel that timed testing is necessary for promoting fact mastery. However, there is no evidence to support this theory. In fact, there is evidence to the contrary. In a study of nearly 300 1st graders, Henry and Brown (2008) found that those students who were more frequently exposed to timed testing actually demonstrated slower progress toward automaticity with their facts than their counterparts who were not tested.

Why are timed tests still so prevalent given the evidence that they don't work? We think many schools continue to use timed testing because they simply do not know how else to assess fact mastery. We hope to rectify this issue and offer a variety of formative assessments in Chapters 6 and 7. These assessment tools and techniques allow teachers to assess all four components of fluency while still encouraging mathematics confidence in their students.

Fundamental 5: Students Need Substantial and Enjoyable Practice

Substantial and enjoyable practice should be considered as an alternative to timed drills for developing mastery with basic facts. Imagine, for example, posing this question to 1st or 2nd grade students: *How many equations can you write that equal 10?* Students enjoy open-ended challenges, and the task allows for natural differentiation, with some students inventing equations with three and four addends and others simply listing known facts. In looking at the ways the students thought about their equations, you learn what number relationships they know—and, as you will soon read, knowing how far numbers are from 10 is an essential concept.

These same students may also play Go Fish for 10s, a game where a match is a combination of 10 (a student with a 4 asks, "Do you have any 6s?"). As you will see later in this book, many familiar games can be adapted to practice basic facts, including Four in a Row, Concentration, and War. We will also share many novel basic fact games, such as Crossed Wires, in which students create grids (arrays) of crossed wires to practice derived fact strategies for multiplication.

Games and other enjoyable challenges provide ample fact practice without constantly using those pages with 100+ facts. Additionally, games are *interactive,* so students can think aloud and hear others' strategies (Bay-Williams & Kling, 2014; Godfrey & Stone, 2013). Think-aloud opportunities are beneficial to all students but are particularly effective with students who traditionally struggle to learn mathematics (Frye et al., 2013; Gersten & Clarke, 2007).

Furthermore, during game play, the teacher has an opportunity to implement formative assessment tools to monitor each student's progress toward mastery. However, it is not enough for a game to be fun; it also has to provide a meaningful mathematics experience. The features described below provide guidance on how to select games that will, in fact, provide effective fact practice. Although a game may not reflect all these features, any game that has most of these features will more effectively help students' fluency development.

10 Questions to Guide Game Selection

To what extent does the game . . .

1. Provide an opportunity to practice the subset of facts that the students are learning?
2. Appeal to the age of your students?
3. Employ visuals or tools (such as ten frames, quick looks, or arrays) to support strategy development?
4. Involve selecting from among derived fact strategies (for mastery-level games)?
5. Provide opportunities for discussion among students about their mathematical thinking?
6. Encourage individual accountability? (For example, are students solving their own facts or competing to solve the same fact? The former practice provides more "think time" and avoids opting out.)
7. Remove time pressures?
8. Involve logic or strategic moves, enhancing the "fun factor"?
9. Offer opportunities for adaptation so that all students can experience appropriate challenge?
10. Lend itself to you being able to listen and watch in order to assess progress?

Sometimes you need a game that is focused on one set of foundational facts (e.g., 5s facts for multiplication); at other times, you need a game that requires that each student identify a derived fact strategy (e.g., deciding how to break apart one factor to use known facts). When working on derived facts, students need think time. Therefore, when selecting a game to help students practice derived fact strategies, a good choice is one in which time is not a factor and where each player is finding a different fact so that students are not trying to find an answer faster than their partner. Once students are automatic with all of their facts, foundational and derived, then games that involve speed may be appropriate and enjoyable. As students get older, the more strategic a game is, the more fun it is to play. Games like Connect Four, for example, involve trying to both get four in a row yourself and block your partner. In summary, good game selection requires various considerations: age of the student, the facts being learned, and student fluency with that set of facts.

Within the covers of this book are more than 40 games that reflect, at least to some extent, the features of effective games described above. Nearly all of these games are readily adaptable to other fact sets or operations, resulting in well over 100 versions that provide enjoyable, targeted, strategy-focused ways to move students toward Phase 3 (mastery). Additionally, many other games exist online and in various books. The features above can be used to evaluate the quality of these games in supporting students' emerging fluency and automaticity.

Let's Get Started!

Hopefully this chapter has piqued your interest for the need to change how fact fluency is developed and assessed. We have a lot of work ahead! By the time you have finished reading this book, you will

- Develop an understanding of foundational facts for each operation.
- Develop an understanding of research-based derived fact strategies for each operation.
- Learn how to sequence facts instruction to best promote natural strategy development and eventual fluency and automaticity.
- Explore activities and games for helping students progress through the phases of fact mastery.
- Consider a variety of assessment tools that can monitor fact mastery in informative and supportive ways.

Let's get started!

2

Foundational Addition and Subtraction Facts

Just as a concrete foundation must be poured before a house can be built, some facts must be known to help solve for other facts. Otherwise, students are left to simple memorization, a practice that has been shown to be ineffective. Fortunately, for most students, foundational fact sets are easier to learn. For example, students understand the concept of "more," having had life experiences asking for more or noticing more ("Can I have one more?" "She has two more than I do!"). Therefore, a good place to begin foundational fact work is with adding and subtracting 0, 1, and 2, followed by encountering the other foundational fact sets highlighted in Figure 2.1.

This chapter will illustrate how foundational facts can be developed from beginning ideas of number and operations, offer suggestions for how to sequence the learning of foundational facts, and provide activities for meaningful practice of foundational facts. We begin by considering the first encounters young students have with number and how those early experiences can be used to foster flexibility and prepare students to engage in learning the foundational facts. As we share in each chapter, this chapter connects to the fundamentals of basic fact fluency in these ways:

1. **Mastery must focus on fluency.** The foundational facts are critical building blocks for the types of fact strategies fluent students create. Thus, students

must develop rich, flexible understandings of the foundational facts discussed in this chapter.

2. **Fluency develops in three phases.** Activities such as quick looks and games are explored to help students move from Phase 1 (counting) to Phase 3 (mastery) of foundational facts.

3. **Foundational facts must precede derived facts.** The foundational facts for addition and subtraction are the focus of this chapter.

4. **Timed tests do not assess fluency.** Monitoring fluency with foundational facts includes noticing if students are quickly counting or actually have automaticity, a distinction that requires better forms of assessment (the focus of Chapter 6).

5. **Students need substantial and enjoyable practice.** Engaging and meaningful games are provided for each set of foundational facts.

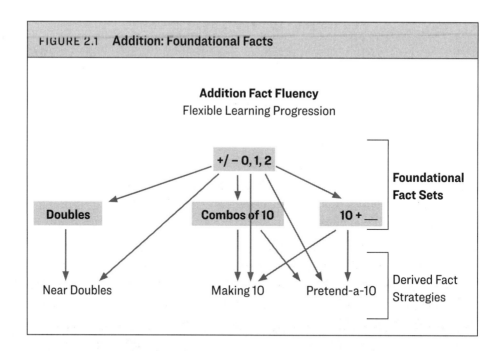

FIGURE 2.1   Addition: Foundational Facts

Early Number Concepts

The beginnings of fluency begin in preschool, a time in which students typically encounter many tactile experiences counting and representing numbers, including the introduction of dot patterns and five frames. *Dot patterns* are arrangements of dots that make visible how a number might be decomposed. A *five frame* is a column (or row, depending on orientation) of five squares in which dots are placed to help students focus on the relationship of numbers with the benchmark of five. Dot patterns and five frames help students learn to decompose numbers in flexible ways and develop visual images of small numbers. Look, for example, at the first dot pattern in Figure 2.2.

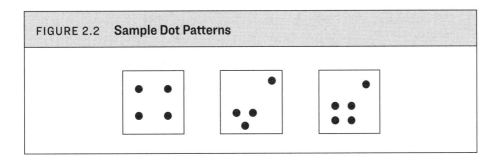

FIGURE 2.2   Sample Dot Patterns

Adults recognize this quantity instantly as four. However, kindergartners generate a variety of responses, such as "I saw a box and knew it was four"; "I saw a square, and it has four corners"; or "I saw 2 and 2, and that makes 4." Some students see the twos horizontally, others see the twos vertically, and inevitably a few even see the twos diagonally.

By extending beyond the most common images of number, teachers can elicit additional ways to decompose a number, as in the second dot pattern in Figure 2.2 (students often see this pattern as 3 and 1). Finally, building on the first image of four, the teacher can present the last image in Figure 2.2. Often referred to as the "giraffe" by students, this image can elicit a key principle of early addition: adding one more to a number. Students recognize the image as 5 because they remembered the image of 4 and simply added one more. This "number-after rule" is key to learning to add by counting on (Baroody, 1995).

To nudge students to recognize these number relationships, it is helpful to present the images using a quick look routine, outlined below.

Step 1: Identify Focus

Strategically select a quick look to focus on the number relation or fact you want children to notice (e.g., combinations of 4).

Select an image that fits your focus (note: do not tell students the focus).

Step 2: Give Quick Looks

Show a quick look for two to three seconds and then hide it.

Repeat for a second two- to three-second look.

Step 3: Talk About How

Ask, "How many did you see?"

Ask, "How did you see the total?" [Elicit many responses and ideas.]

Step 4: Connect Symbols

Not initially, but eventually (later kindergarten or 1st grade), ask:

"What number sentence could match this quick look?"

"How can we write that addition fact?"

Step 3, Talk About How, is essential for helping students develop greater flexibility with numbers as they hear their peers share different ways of thinking about quantities. Keeping the image visible as students talk will enable them to point at the dots, if needed, to support their explanations and will help all students make sense of the discussion. Repeat with other images (typically four to six) as time allows. Keep in mind that the quality of the discussion is more important than the quantity of images shown.

Over the course of a year, use quick looks within a variety of formats (dot patterns, five frames, ten frames, etc.). This will expose students to many different representations of a number. As students discuss their strategies for determining the quantity in the image, they learn to move beyond counting what they see, as illustrated in this vignette.

A preschool class is sitting together on the carpet. The teacher holds up the five frame (Figure 2.3) for two seconds, hides it, and repeats the process.

Then the teacher begins a class discussion by asking her students how many they saw and how they saw it.

Teacher: How many dots did you see? I see a lot of people holding up four fingers. Miguel, how did you see it?

Miguel: I counted four in my head.

Teacher: Did anyone else do that? Okay, how about another way? Did anyone see it a different way? Mia?

Mia: I knew it was four because I'm 5 now, but when I was 4 I knew that's what four looks like.

Teacher: Oh, I see—you remember what it looked like because you used to be 4. How about Javon?

Javon: I saw two here (points at card) and two there (points), and I know two and two make four.

Teacher: Thank you, Javon. How about someone else? Simone, how did you see it?

Simone: I saw there was one missing . . .

Teacher: Can you tell us more?

Simone: I knew there were five, but one was missing, so now there are four.

FIGURE 2.3   Sample Five Frame for Quick Look

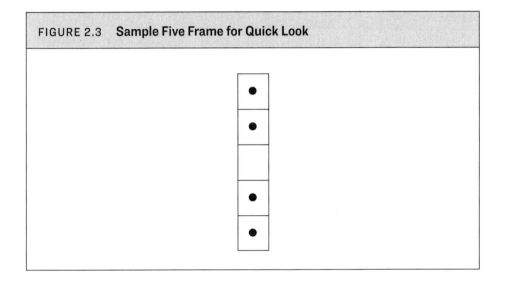

This teacher is using a quick look routine to encourage her young students to develop the ability to subitize—to recognize a quantity without counting the individual items. Caldwell, Kobett, and Karp (2014) describe subitizing as one of four critical components of early numeracy because it deepens students' understanding of cardinality and encourages flexibility with part-whole relationships. Many researchers recommend that students develop counting and subitizing skills simultaneously so they do not become overly dependent on counting and can see numbers as units that can be decomposed into smaller units (Clements, 1999; Wheatley and Reynolds, 1999). The type of thinking that students use when subitizing—breaking the images into smaller chunks that they can recognize and mentally manipulate—is the thinking students apply to learning basic facts. Thus, subitizing is an important precursor to eventual fact fluency. Learning to subitize is supported through frequent experiences with quick looks.

Tools for Representing Numbers Flexibly

Picture the dot arrangements you see on a regular die. Although you can instantly recognize these quantities, if they were the only images of the numbers 1–6 you had ever seen, you would not have had the opportunity to think about a number, like 5, in a variety of ways. Similarly, students need experiences representing numbers in a variety of ways. Flexibly decomposing and recomposing numbers within 10 is a key focus in the early grades. Tools such as five frames and ten frames can facilitate this, but *we must represent, and encourage students to represent, numbers on the frames in a variety of ways.*

Consider for a moment all the different ways you could represent the number 8 on a ten frame. Take a moment to think of several ways and then look at Figure 2.4.

Some students (or teachers) feel they must fill one column of 5 (or row, depending on orientation) of the ten frame before placing any counters in the other column. Although this may help students recognize how quantities relate to the anchor numbers 5 and 10, it also restricts their flexibility to see a number in a variety of ways. By *not* limiting how we fill ten frames, a wide variety of representations for a given number can be discovered and discussed, providing a great opportunity for developing number sense and early fact practice, as shown in Figure 2.4.

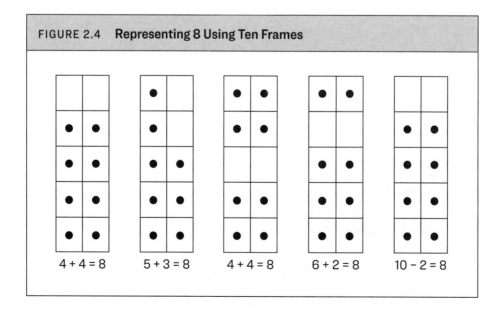

FIGURE 2.4   **Representing 8 Using Ten Frames**

4 + 4 = 8   5 + 3 = 8   4 + 4 = 8   6 + 2 = 8   10 − 2 = 8

Having students represent and discuss various ways of constructing a number on a ten frame is a wonderful activity for thinking about how to decompose it. Such physical representations of ten frames prepare students to make sense of quantities, which in turn leads to more sophisticated ways of recognizing the quantities. An example is shown in the final image of Figure 2.4, which focuses on the important idea of "how far from 10." Finally, you might have noticed that the orientation of these ten frames is vertical, rather than horizontal. Both orientations support subitizing, just as equations can be written horizontally or vertically. Feel free to vary your orientation—if anything, it just encourages more flexibility!

Early Understanding of Operations: Storytelling

The integration of frequent use of quick looks may be a departure from your own memories of early childhood mathematics. Similarly, how story problems are used in learning mathematics has changed (or needs to change). Story problems have a history of being introduced after skills are learned, often at the end of a long section of exercises. This approach has several shortcomings. First, it places the concrete context provided by the stories after the abstract representation of the mathematics, despite significant research that suggests that beginning with the concrete and moving to the abstract is more effective (Carpenter, Fennema, Franke, Levi, & Empson, 2014; National Research Council, 2001). Second, when stories follow exercises, they tend to be solved using the skill just practiced. Students figure this out quickly and stop reading the problems, simply extracting the numbers they see and performing the computation. Hence, they fail to develop the ability to comprehend and solve more complicated mathematics story problems (Schoenfeld, 1991; Verschaffel, Greer, & De Corte, 2000).

In contrast, instruction should begin with story problems. Research shows that even students in kindergarten can solve problems involving addition, subtraction, multiplication, and division if problems are set in a familiar context and tools are available to model what occurs in the story (Carpenter, Ansell, Franke, Fennema, & Weisbeck, 1993; National Research Council, 2001). For example, kindergartners might be presented with a problem like this:

> Toto the dog has 3 squeaky toys. Her family gives her 2 more toys. How many toys does Toto have now?

Students can use counters, drawings, or acting to model the action in the story and conclude that Toto now has five toys. Note that this problem can be solved without calling it an "addition problem" or using symbols such as the plus sign (+); thus, it is reasonable to present such problems prior to introducing the operation formally. Eventually the stories and the visualizations are connected to more symbolic representations of the operation. As such, story problems have a secondary benefit: fact practice. Consistent use of a variety of story problems beginning in kindergarten is an important component in fluency development. A student might make a drawing to represent Toto's toys and share her work, and the class can talk about how they see the five toys in her illustration.

The way in which a story is told matters. Carpenter and colleagues (2014) have presented three types of addition and subtraction story problems, which we briefly describe here.

Type 1: Action. Many story problems have some sort of action involved, where the quantity either increases or decreases due to that action. Sometimes these are called "join" or "separate" stories, including in the Common Core State Standards (2010). Consider this story:

> Toto has 5 bones in her doggie bowl. She eats 2 of the bones. How many bones are in her bowl now?

In the story about Toto presented previously, the number of toys increased. In this story, however, the quantity of bones decreases due to the action of Toto eating two of them. In both stories, an action occurred (something came or something left). Action problems such as these are generally easiest for students to solve because they can be modeled with counters or drawings. However, changing what is unknown in the problem can change the level of challenge:

> Toto has some bones in her doggie bowl. She eats 2 bones. Now she has 4. How many bones did Toto start with?

Because the students do not have a starting quantity to represent, this problem is much harder than the first two examples. This story can be written as a missing addend equation or a subtraction equation, helping students see the relationship between addition and subtraction. Thus, these story types are important in helping students learn basic subtraction facts (in this case, $4 - 2 = 2$).

Type 2: Part-part-whole. Some stories do not involve direct action but instead involve separate sets. Consider this problem:

> The Klash softball team has 9 players on the field and 2 players in the dugout. How many players are on the team?

There are two separate sets in this story: players on the field and players in the dugout. There is no action joining or separating those sets; they are simply there.

Together, these two distinct parts make up a whole (the entire team), leading to the classification of this problem as a part-part-whole story. Variations on part-part-whole problems that increase difficulty level include (1) providing only one part and the whole or (2) providing only the whole, which usually offers several viable combinations of parts that students can determine. Examples of this second variation will be shared later in this chapter.

Type 3: Comparison. A comparison story involves no action but instead requires the student to compare two different sets:

> A basket contains 8 red apples and 5 green apples. How many more red apples are there than green apples?

Students can create models to help them make sense of comparison stories. For example, to solve this problem, a student might use snap cubes to create a model like the one shown in Figure 2.5.

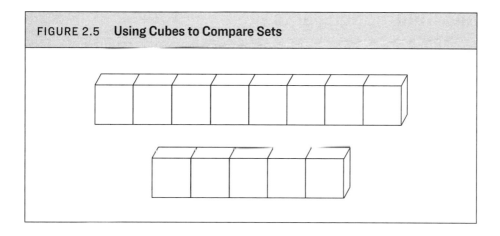

FIGURE 2.5   **Using Cubes to Compare Sets**

Here, the numbers of cubes or the lengths of the models are compared to determine the number of excess red apples. Also, in a comparison situation, the student must sometimes consider the distance between the numbers. Thinking about subtraction as a comparison of some sort is different than taking away and is also very important in developing fluency with the basic facts for subtraction.

We introduce these story types because they help students understand critical number relationships concretely. When students understand subtraction as both taking away and comparing, they can decide which idea is more useful in solving the problem. To solve 11 – 9, for example, it is easy to see that the numbers are 2 apart because they are close together, which negates the need to take away 9. Conversely, if the basic fact is 8 – 1, a take-away approach makes more sense than comparing the distance between the numbers. As an adult, you may naturally toggle between these two ideas, but if students are only exposed to subtraction as taking away, they will not be able to apply the idea of comparing.

Furthermore, stories help students make sense of the commutative and associative properties, which are both necessary for fact mastery. Toto has five toys whether you add the old to the new or the new to the old (3 + 2 = 2 + 3). If you move one of his new toys over to the pile of his old toys, you still have 5 toys. Finally, please note that this brief discussion of story problem types is for your information as the teacher. It is not necessary or recommended that students attempt to "label" various story problem types.

A Progression for Foundational Addition and Subtraction Facts

Story problems and activities representing numbers with dot patterns, five frames, and ten frames provide a setting rich for the introduction and practice of basic facts. Figure 2.1 (see p. 14) illustrates the flexible learning progression that leads to addition fact fluency, showing that the sets of facts at the bottom of the figure require or benefit from the fact sets above. The groups of foundational facts in the middle of the progression (doubles, combinations of 10, and 10 + ____ facts) can be practiced simultaneously; it is not necessary to master one of these groups before introducing one of the others. However, automaticity with all four fact sets should be obtained before teaching derived addition and subtraction fact strategies. Throughout the rest of this chapter, we will discuss each foundational fact set and share activities and games that can be used for meaningful practice.

Adding or Subtracting 0, 1, or 2

The first group of facts to master (i.e., get to Phase 3 or develop automaticity) involves adding or subtracting 0, 1, or 2. This is because these facts relate closely to the counting sequence. For example, adding 1 gives the next number in the counting sequence; subtracting 1 gives the number before. Visual tools such as number lines are especially helpful for connecting these facts to the counting sequence, as shown in the activities described here.

Stories. Story problems provide an important context for practicing the 0s, 1s, and 2s facts. Many real-world contexts naturally involve adding or subtracting 1 or 2; however, the use of stories is especially important for helping students make sense of the meaning of adding or subtracting 0. It is important to go beyond simply teaching a rule like "adding or subtracting 0 keeps the number the same"; instead, teachers should encourage students to use the meaning of the operation to understand *why* this is true. Consider this problem:

> There are 3 pencils in my desk and 0 pencils in my backpack. How many pencils do I have in all?

Students can use their understanding of addition as putting groups together to reason that 3 + 0 = 3 because the second group, the pencils in the backpack, doesn't contribute any pencils to the total.

Meaningful practice can also be provided using more open-ended story problems:

> I have 5 apples in all. Some apples are red. Some are yellow. How many of each might I have?

As they begin exploring problems like this, students may find it helpful to use red and yellow counters to help them model the different possibilities. Teachers can challenge students to find as many solutions as possible, recording the pairs of numbers they found. Some students will need time to manipulate the counters to generate just one possibility, while other students may quickly recognize a pattern and use it to generate all combinations without models. Some students may even be able to argue how they know they have found all possible combinations. Thus, this task has the potential to challenge students of varying ability levels. It is also easily adaptable to new contexts and a new total (e.g., "I have 10 crayons in all. Some are green, some are purple. How many of each might I have?") and can provide continued opportunities for fact practice throughout the year.

Quick looks. Carefully sequencing quick look images can provide valuable practice adding or subtracting 0, 1, or 2. For example, following the first image in Figure 2.2 (see p. 15) with the last image in Figure 2.2 can invoke the idea of adding 1 more: 4 + 1 = 5. Similarly, showing an image of a full five frame followed by an image of a five frame with two empty spaces can encourage students to think of 5 − 2 = 3. The key is carefully selecting and sequencing images to encourage students to decompose small quantities in flexible ways.

Games. Games provide opportunities for meaningful practice. The game Sleeping Bears can be used as early as preschool to encourage students to find various ways to decompose small quantities and relate them to the number 5. This can be adapted to 10 as children progress to kindergarten and 1st grade.

GAME 1

SLEEPING BEARS

● ● ● ●

For each pair of players, you need: five teddy bear counters, a plastic cup or bowl (for the "cave"), a five frame

How to play: One student places some of the bears in the "cave," pretending they are taking a nap. The other student looks at the bears that are "awake" (unhidden) and tries to figure out how many bears are "sleeping" (hidden). By placing the unhidden bears on the five frame, the student is encouraged to recognize and utilize combinations of numbers that make five (see Figure 2.6).

Possible variations: Use a different number of bears. Ask older students to write equations to represent the bears that are sleeping and the bears that are awake.

In the Racing Bears games that follow, students roll dice and add or subtract the numbers. Ask students to say or write equations to match so that they make the connection between the movement of the bears (concrete) and the equation (abstract).

FIGURE 2.6   **Preschoolers Playing Sleeping Bears with Five Frames**

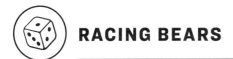

RACING BEARS
● ● ● ●

For each pair of players, you need: two number lines from 0–10 (or a game board with squares labeled 0–10) to be a "racetrack" (one for each student), two plastic bears (one for each student), a die labeled as described for the desired version

Game 2: Bears Race to 10
Label the sides of a die +0, +0, +1, +1, +2, and +2. Students start their bears at 0. They then take turns rolling the die and moving their bear the appropriate number of spaces. The first bear to 10 wins the race.

Game 3: Bears Race to 0
Label the sides of a die −0, −0, −1, −1, −2, and −2. Students start their bears at 10. They then take turns rolling the die and moving their bear down the number line the appropriate number of spaces. The first bear to 0 wins the race.

Game 4: Bears Race to Escape
Label the sides of a die −0, +0, −1, +1, −2, and +2. Students start their bears at 5. They then take turns rolling the die and moving their bear the appropriate number of spaces up or down the number line. The first bear to "escape" the number line by reaching 0 or 10 wins the race.

Possible variation: Use a vertical number line and adapt the names of the games to Bears Climb Up/Down the Tree.

Doubles

Although no one is sure why, research has shown that students can more easily master their doubles combinations (2 + 2 = 4, 3 + 3 = 6, etc.) than most other groups of facts (National Research Council, 2001). This ease of mastery, combined with the observation that more difficult facts (such as 7 + 8) are close to doubles facts, make the doubles a particularly useful group of foundational facts to learn.

Stories and quick looks. Students can first become familiar with doubles through quick look images that show matching pairs and through story problems involving doubles, as shown in Figure 2.7.

Perhaps one reason students remember doubles facts so easily is because there are so many examples of doubles naturally occurring in the world. Two hands with five fingers on each makes a doubles fact: 5 + 5 = 10. The front wheels and back wheels of a car also make a doubles fact: 2 + 2 = 4. The two rows of eggs in a standard egg carton form yet another doubles fact: 6 + 6 = 12. Teachers can harness the potential of naturally occurring doubles in story problems, even asking students to sketch their own pictures of doubles situations in real life or make up their own stories involving doubles facts. Introductory experiences with doubles in natural contexts and dot pattern or ten frame images can provide a meaningful backdrop to introduce the term *doubles fact*. Once doubles facts have been formally identified, additional practice will be needed to ensure that students master them.

FIGURE 2.7	Ways to Introduce Students to Doubles Facts	
Image for 3 + 3 = 6	**Image for 4 + 4 = 8**	**Story problem for 8 + 8**
(dot pattern)	(ten frame)	Ben has a new crayon box that has 8 crayons in the top row and 8 crayons in the bottom row. How many crayons does Ben have in all?

Games. The three games described here are designed for meaningful practice of addition doubles. Doubles Match-Up encourages the context-to-equation connection, while Doubles Bingo provides additional experiences with doubling a number.

GAME 5

DOUBLES MATCH-UP

For groups of one to three players, you need: a deck of doubles pictures (photos/clip art of things that occur naturally in the world, such two rows of six eggs in an egg carton), and a deck of doubles facts number sentences that match the figures (e.g., 6 + 6 = 12)

How to play: Spread all the cards out, faceup. Students take turns finding a picture and corresponding equation and explaining why it is a match.

Possible variations: Play as a memory game, where all cards are turned upside down; students take turns turning over two cards at a time, attempting to find a matching pair. Provide the pictures only and ask students to write their own number sentences to match. (For older grades, this could include addition and multiplication equations.)

GAME 6

DOUBLES BINGO   ● ● ● ●

For the whole class, you need: one blank 4 × 4 bingo card per student, 16 bingo chips per student, one deck of cards with kings and jacks removed (ace = 1, queen = 0)

How to play: Provide a list of the doubles sums: 0, 2, 4, 6, 8, 10, 12, 14, 16, 18, and 20. Each student fills in a blank 4 × 4 bingo card, writing a number from this list in each space. Some sums will need to be repeated, and not all sums must be used. To begin play, draw a card from the deck. Students must use that card to make an addition doubles fact. For example, if a 4 is drawn, students find the answer to 4 + 4 and cover the doubles sum (8) on their cards. Only one space can be covered on each turn, and students cannot move a bingo chip after it has been placed. Four chips in a row (horizontally, diagonally, or vertically) results in a bingo.

Possible variations: Use a 5 × 5 bingo card. Adapt the game to any fact set by simply giving the students the list of possible sums. For example, students can play Two Less Bingo to practice the −2 facts, using a card deck with only 2–10 and a bingo card with the numbers 0–8.

Combinations of 10

Research over the past few decades has brought to light the necessity of focusing on the combinations of 10 (2 + 8, 3 + 7, 4 + 6, etc.) during the early years of school. International studies have shown that combinations of 10 have traditionally been a major focus in countries that consistently top the list in mathematical achievement (Fuson & Kwon, 1992). As a result, combinations of 10 are becoming a much stronger component of kindergarten and 1st grade curricula in the United States.

Stories. The ten frame presents a natural tool for helping students identify combinations of 10. For example, students can use ten frames and counters to generate as many solutions as possible to story problems such as the following:

A neighborhood has 10 pets. Some of the pets are cats, and some of them are dogs. How many of each pet could there be?

Students might use counters of one color to represent the cats and counters of another color to represent the dogs, using the structure of the ten frame to ensure they have a total of 10 pets. The game 10 Sleeping Bears can be played on the ten frame to learn combinations of 10.

GAME 7

10 SLEEPING BEARS   ● ● ● ●

For each pair of players, you need: one ten frame, 10 plastic bears (or other counters), one cup or bowl (for the "cave")

How to play: This game is played like Sleeping Bears, described in Game 1. Students have 10 bears, placing some in the cave and the rest in the ten frame. Their partners use the ten frame to see how many bears are awake and then figure out how many bears must be sleeping.

Possible variation: Provide students with a recording table to keep track of the number of bears that are awake and sleeping each round, to reinforce the number combinations that equal 10.

Bears Awake	Bears Sleeping

Quick looks. Using quick looks with ten frames can also facilitate learning combinations of 10, particularly when the ten frame is nearly full. For example, showing 8 on the ten frame might invoke thinking of the complement, 10 − 2 = 8, as it is easier for some students to recognize what is missing than to recognize how many dots are present. Drawing attention to this strategy when it is shared can help students internalize the combination 2 + 8 = 10.

Games. Many classic games can be adapted to creating a combination of 10. Memory, for example, can be adapted to look for combinations that equal 10 (rather than numbers that match). Game 8 describes an adaptation of a game loved by 1st and 2nd grade students—Go Fish.

GAME 8
GO FISH FOR 10s ● ● ● ●

For two to four players, you need: one deck of numeral cards or playing cards with kings and jacks removed (ace = 1, queen = 0)

How to play: Play like the card game Go Fish, but instead of looking for matching cards, students look for combinations of 10. Players each receive four cards that they can look at but do not let the other players see. First, each player looks for combinations of 10 in their four cards. These pairs are laid down on the table for all to see, and additional cards are drawn from the "fish pond" (draw pile) so that each student always has four cards. Students take turns asking each other for a specific card. For example, if a boy has a 4 in his hand, he would ask another player, "Do you have a 6?" The player either hands over the requested card or says, "Go Fish." Students continue to draw cards to keep four in their hands. Play continues until all cards are used. At the end of the game, students can share or record the number sentences for their combinations of 10.

Possible variations: Play with three or five cards in a hand. Change the sum to any amount within 10, such as Go Fish for 8s, using only cards 0–8. Use for subtraction. For example, Go Fish for 2s can require students to look for cards that have a difference of two, such as matching an 8 with a 6 or a 10.

Students also need to know combinations of 10s to find missing addends, as in 9 + ___ = 10 or 7 + ___ = 10. This is the type of thinking behind the Making 10 and

Pretend-a-10 strategies, where students must know how many are needed to make 10 or how far away a number is from 10. Games such as Erase are particularly useful for developing this understanding.

GAME 9
ERASE

● ● ● ●

For two to four players, you need: seven 10-sided dice and a cup, a deck of numeral cards, or playing cards with values 0–10 (ace = 1, queen = 0), calculators

How to play: Play like the classic game Sevens. Players take turns rolling all seven dice or turning over seven cards, adding the seven numbers to get their score. However, if the student finds a combination of 10, those numbers are "erased" (removed) and not counted into the score. The player with the lowest score wins.

Example:

1. A student rolls 4, 5, 6, 5, 8, 9, and 3.

2. The student pairs 4 and 6 and 5 and 5, because they are combinations of 10.

3. The student's score is the sum of the numbers that are left: 8 + 9 + 3 = 20. (Students may use a calculator to add the remaining values, if needed.)

Possible variations: Change the sum to 7 and use regular dice. Use fewer dice or cards. Designate a wild card (such as a king or queen) so that more pairs can be made.

10 + _____ Facts

Understanding that a teen number comprises a 10 and some number of units is a key goal in early elementary school and essential for eventually using the Making 10 and Pretend-a-10 strategies.

One way to encourage students to recognize this concept is by having them represent teen numbers on a double ten frame (see Figure 2.8).

Stories and visuals. A context for exploring 10 + ____ facts might be filling boxes of pencils, with each box holding 10 pencils, or exploring money combinations (dimes and pennies). For example, you might have students use pennies on a double ten frame to help them solve this problem.

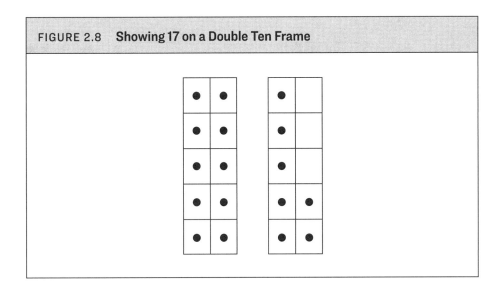

FIGURE 2.8   **Showing 17 on a Double Ten Frame**

My cousin has 15 pennies. She wants to trade some pennies for a dime. How many dimes and pennies could she have after she trades?

Repeat the story several times with different teen numbers. After this, encourage students to share any patterns they may have noticed in the ten frames, eliciting the idea that they can easily keep one ten frame full to show the 10 (or the pennies to be exchanged for a dime) and then change the quantity shown on the other ten frame to match the units of the new teen number. Support this thinking by writing corresponding equations, such as 15 = 10 + 5, to make the 10 + _____ fact explicit.

Once the concept has been introduced, place value tools such as snap cubes or base ten blocks can also be used for exploring teen numbers. Encourage students to find two different ways to manipulate the tools to represent given teen numbers. For example, students might represent the number 14 with base ten blocks by using either one rod and four cubes or 14 cubes. They might represent 14 with coins by using either 14 pennies or one dime and four pennies. Encouraging students to relate the two representations can help them recognize the relationship between the teen numbers and adding numbers to 10.

Games. Once again, Memory can easily be adapted for this new group of facts. For Memory, simply create pairs of cards using the expressions (e.g., 10 + 4) and corresponding sums (14). Also, Square Deal is designed specifically for meaningful practice of 10 + _____ facts.

GAME 10

SQUARE DEAL

● ● ● ●

For partners, you need: ten frame cards, some with full frames and some partially filled frames, or a deck of cards with kings and jacks removed (ace = 1, queen = 0); two colors of chips to cover game board (or two colors of markers if board is laminated); Square Deal game board (which can be laminated for reuse)

19	17	11	12	13
12	14	15	14	11
18	19	16	17	12
19	17	11	12	13
15	10	13	16	14

Before play, separate full ten frames from those representing units.

How to play: Player 1 draws from each pile (10s and units) and selects a square on the game board that matches the sum. For example, drawing a 10 and 3 allows the student to select any cell with a 13 on it. Student says aloud, "10 plus 3 equals 13" and places a chip on a 13. Player 1 returns both cards to the bottoms of their respective piles. Repeat for Player 2. The goal is to cover four spots that make a square. The winner is the student who can cover the most squares. (Can they overlap? You decide!)

Possible variations: Cover four in a row, instead of making squares. Use this game board for derived facts by separating the deck into two stacks at random, instead of isolating 10s and units. If two numbers are drawn that yield a sum not on the board, the player loses a turn.

Summary

Meaningful practice with all foundational facts throughout the first few years of school is essential. This includes solving different kinds of story problems, using quick looks to encourage mental decomposition of numbers, and playing games with the clear expectation to "think aloud while you play." Although you may be introducing one group of foundational facts at a time, you should think cumulatively, blending the focus on the new group with continued practice with the other types of foundational facts. Furthermore, it is important to look for opportunities to make connections to the related subtraction facts. For example, as the students play Go Fish for 10s, have them ask themselves questions like "What do I need to add to 7 to make 10?" Help them to see that they can also represent this question by writing $10 - 7 = ?$.

Finally, as students are engaging in these activities, take advantage of the opportunity to observe their thinking. Tools to help you monitor and track students' mastery of the foundational facts is the focus of Chapter 6.

3

Derived Fact Strategies for Addition and Subtraction

For decades, many well-meaning teachers and parents have been quick to put addition and subtraction flash cards into the hands of their students. A major reason why a drill-based approach to instruction is less effective is that it involves memorization of isolated facts, and learning and retaining anything without connecting it to other knowledge is difficult. This is illustrated in the following activity, adapted from Baroody (2006).

- Set a timer for 15 seconds.
- Attempt to memorize this number: 25811141720.
- Close this book and attempt to recall the number.

Were you able to memorize the number? Rote memorization often requires time and effort, and even if you were able to memorize the number, how likely is it that you will still remember it tomorrow? Compare this experience with attempting to remember the sequence in a meaningful way, such as looking for a relationship between subsequent numbers. In this example, the pattern simply starts at 2 and adds 3 to the previous number (2 + 3 = 5, 5 + 3 = 8, 8 + 3 = 11, etc.). Now you can likely recall this number after 15 seconds, 15 minutes, or even 15 days! As this example shows, making connections greatly enhances learning and retention, and addition and subtraction facts form a terrain that is rich with potential connections.

The five fundamental ideas presented in Chapter 1 are also reflected in this chapter.

1. **Mastery must focus on fluency.** Derived fact strategies for addition and subtraction require a focus on strategy selection and flexibility.
2. **Fluency develops in three phases.** This chapter assumes students have obtained Phase 3 (mastery) with most of their foundational facts. It is now time to focus on developing fluency with the rest of the addition and subtraction facts. This requires that extensive time be devoted to developing strategies (Phase 2), the major focus of this chapter.
3. **Foundational facts must precede derived facts.** Students use the foundational facts they have mastered (Phase 3) to develop derived fact strategies for addition and subtraction.
4. **Timed tests do not assess fluency.** Timed tests provide no data on which derived fact strategies a student is able to use, how efficiently the student applies the strategy, or which strategies the student prefers to use. Time pressures also work against strategy learning, as thinking through strategies *initially* takes longer than counting.
5. **Students need substantial and enjoyable practice.** The numerous strategy games offered in this chapter provide practice with choosing and using derived fact strategies.

Addition Derived Fact Strategies

Once students have automaticity (Phase 3) with the foundational facts, they are ready to find any addition or subtraction fact within 20, using a derived fact strategy (Phase 2). The connections between the foundational facts and the derived fact strategies are illustrated in Figure 3.1.

Note that the derived fact strategies *require* the use of these foundational facts. If you are not sure if your students have automaticity with the foundational facts, consider using the assessment tools in Chapter 6 to determine readiness.

In this chapter, we will explore how to engage students in learning three addition fact strategies in meaningful ways. Students may invent other strategies, but the three strategies of Near Doubles, Making 10, and Pretend-a-10 are accessible, commonly used, and powerful, making explicit instruction important. A range of studies comparing strategy-focused interventions to non-strategy-focused comparison groups show that strategy groups outperform their peers on using strategies as well as on automaticity and accuracy (i.e., they are more fluent!) (Baroody et al., 2016; Locuniak & Jordan, 2008; Purpura et al., 2016; Tournaki, 2003). Importantly, a strategy approach has also consistently shown increased *retention* of learned facts (Baroody, Bajwa, & Eiland, 2009; Henry & Brown, 2008; Hiebert & Carpenter, 1992; Hiebert & Lefevre, 1986; Jordan, Kaplan, Nabors Olah, & Locuniak, 2006). It is also well established that strategy instruction is more effective with children with disabilities than drill and practice (Dennis, Sorrells, & Falcomata, 2016; Gersten et al., 2009; Montague, 1997; Myers & Thornton, 1977; Swanson, 1990; Tournaki, 2003). Such a body of research is convincing: Effective teaching of addition and subtraction facts must be based on explicit strategy instruction.

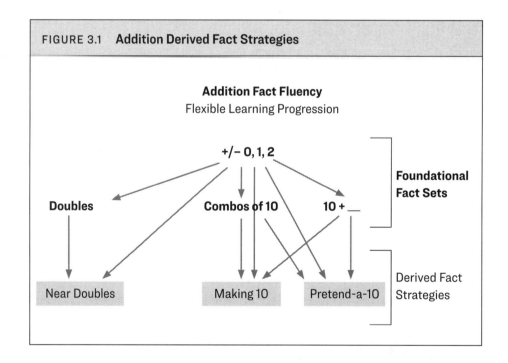

FIGURE 3.1   Addition Derived Fact Strategies

Like the set of foundational facts, derived fact strategies emerge from making connections to stories and visual images like those provided in quick looks. Because the story scenarios for derived addition facts follow the same style as those presented in Chapter 2, we will not continue to provide examples. However, with derived fact strategies, it becomes critically important to focus on thinking through the process, using the think-aloud approach. Therefore, for each strategy, we will share the mental process a student is likely to apply when using that strategy.

Near Doubles

Fairly early in elementary school, children begin to acquire many doubles facts, such as 2 + 2, 4 + 4, and 5 + 5. Thus, students can be encouraged to work from a known doubles fact to derive a harder, related fact. For example, they may solve 6 + 7 by starting from the doubles fact 6 + 6 = 12 and adding 1 more to get 13. Alternately, they may start from 7 + 7 = 14 and subtract 1 to get 13. Such work is at the heart of Phase 2 in the progression toward fact mastery. We refer to this type of thinking as a Near Doubles strategy, because students find a fact that is nearby a double by using a doubles "helper fact." Figure 3.2 shows what the mental process looks like.

FIGURE 3.2   Near Doubles Mental Process

Mental Process in Symbols	What Students Might Think or Say as They Solve
9 + 8 = ___	These numbers are close to each other, so I can use a double.
(8 + 8) + 1 = ___	I'll use 8 + 8. I know this is 16.
8 + 8 = 16, so 9 + 8 = 17.	I know that 8 + 8 equals 16, so 9 + 8 is one more, 17.

What does this process tell us about the mathematics embedded in the strategy? Students need to have mastered two sets of foundational facts (+/- 1 and doubles) to generate the mental reasoning used in the example. Thinking through a strategy takes time, so *slow down*. Students need processing time. If activities are timed, they will resort to counting.

Naming the strategy. Although some resources also identify the Near Doubles strategy, there are others that separate this derived fact strategy into two: Doubles Plus One and Doubles Minus One. We do not make this distinction because we have consistently found that, given any fact that is near a double, some students choose a greater doubles fact and subtract, while others choose the lesser doubles fact and add. Furthermore, some students use a doubles-related strategy that fits neither Doubles Plus One nor Doubles Minus One. Instead, they consider both nearby doubles and choose the number in between the sums. For example, for 8 + 9, they will recall that 8 + 8 = 16 while 9 + 9 = 18, so 8 + 9 must have a sum of 17, since that is the number in between. The strategy name Near Doubles casts a wide enough net to include *all* the ways that students use a doubles fact as a foundation to reason about solving another basic fact.

Similarly, students can use a Near Doubles strategy to solve facts that are two away from a double, (e.g., 6 + 8 or 9 + 7). Again, they may start from the lesser double and add two, start from the greater double and subtract 2, or apply a "sharing" strategy, where the greater addend "gives 1" to the lesser addend to create a double. A student's reasoning might look or sound like the example shown in Figure 3.3.

FIGURE 3.3 **Two Away from a Double Reasoning**	
Mental Process in Symbols	**What Students Might Think or Say as They Solve**
6 + 8 = ?	These two numbers are both close to 7.
$6^7 + 8^7$	I can move one from the 8 over to the 6 and think 7 + 7.
7 + 7 = 14, so 6 + 8 = 14	I know that 7 + 7 equals 14, so 6 + 8 equals 14.

Using quick looks. The Near Doubles strategy is quite intuitive for some students. As they near the end of the kindergarten year, a small handful of students may even create this strategy for facts such as 3 + 4 or 5 + 4. However, those students are the exception. Research has shown that not all students will spontaneously create derived fact strategies like Near Doubles (Henry & Brown, 2008). It is therefore important to provide opportunities for students to discover such strategies, and one effective means for doing so is through carefully selected quick look images. The following process supports building a strong connection between visual images and the related number fact, helping students "see" doubles in near double sums.

Step 1: Show a doubles image followed by a related near doubles image, as shown in Figure 3.4.

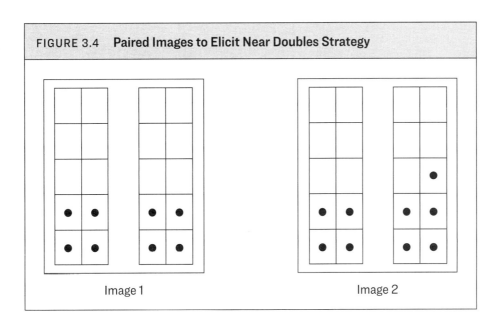

FIGURE 3.4   **Paired Images to Elicit Near Doubles Strategy**

Image 1   Image 2

The first image is presented using the quick looks routine: Students discuss what they saw and how they saw it, following the process outlined in Chapter 2. Repeat this process with the second image. Although students are likely to use a variety of strategies, at least some will describe recalling the previous image's doubles fact of 4 + 4 = 8 and adding one more for the additional dot in the new image. Sequencing the cards in this way facilitates the recognition of the nearby doubles fact that can help them with the second image. Students can then be prompted to try that strategy for themselves on the next set of cards, as a new related pair is shown.

Step 2: Show a near doubles image without a previous doubles image (Figure 3.5).

The next step in encouraging students to internalize the Near Doubles strategy is to show images that are close to doubles facts without showing the related doubles facts at all. In this example, some students might describe hiding one dot on the left-hand ten frame, starting from 5 + 5 = 10, and then adding back the additional dot. Alternately, they might imagine that there is an extra dot present, starting from 6 + 6 = 12 and then removing the additional dot to reach 11.

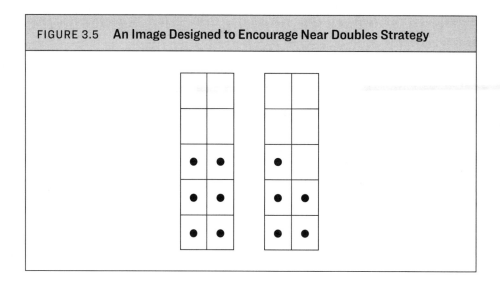

FIGURE 3.5   **An Image Designed to Encourage Near Doubles Strategy**

It is important to allow students to share a variety of strategies for any given image, as opposed to coaching them to strictly use Near Doubles. However, explicit attention can be given to the Near Doubles strategy once it emerges, for example, by asking a student to repeat her explanation of the strategy or by asking all students to try that strategy on the next image.

Step 3: Connect images to symbols by recording strategies in words and number sentences.

Although quick looks with double ten frames are highly effective for eliciting the Near Doubles strategy, how many students walk around with a ten frame in their back pockets? Eventually, it is necessary to help students bridge the gap between the visual and the symbolic representations of this strategy. This can be done by modeling the use of number sentences and words to capture the students' thinking. For example, for Figure 3.5, a student may describe imagining an extra dot to make the double 6 + 6 = 12 and then subtracting that extra dot to get 11. The teacher might model this by recording these number sentences as the student gives the explanation.

6 + 6 = 12

12 − 1 = 11, so

6 + 5 = 11

Eventually, students can be encouraged to take over the work of recording their strategies in either (or both) number sentences and written words. This step facilitates their transition to applying this same type of thinking when given just the fact 6 + 5 without an accompanying visual aid.

Step 4: Connect facts to mental images.

This is actually the reverse of Step 3: beginning with the numerical expression and inviting students to picture a quick look image. *This step is critical!* You may have had the experience of students applying a strategy when they see a visual image, but they don't transfer that thinking to finding the same fact represented as a numerical expression. This may be because we failed to help them connect back to the images we were using to develop the strategy. Therefore, a final step is to invite students to close their eyes and picture a double ten frame whenever they need to apply the strategic thinking they have previously developed.

Making 10 and Pretend-a-10

These two strategies are grouped together because they both focus on the idea of 10. The quick looks for these two approaches are also interchangeable; however, since the reasoning is different, each strategy is described separately.

Making 10. The Making 10 strategy relies on two groups of foundational facts: the combinations of 10 and the 10 + __ facts. In addition, students must also be able to decompose numbers within 10 because, if they are given a sum where one addend is close to 10 (such as 7, 8, or 9), they might need to decompose the other addend to complete a combination of 10. Figure 3.6 shares a student's thinking to highlight the foundational facts that underlie the reasoning.

FIGURE 3.6 **Making 10 Strategy Reasoning**	
Mental Process in Symbols	**What Students Might Think or Say as They Solve**
8 + 7 = __	8 is 2 away from 10. I will use the Making 10 strategy and move 2 over from the 7.
8 + 2 + __ = ?	If I break apart 7 into 2 and some more, what is left?
8 + 2 + 5 = ?	Now I make 10 (add 8 and 2) and then add on the 5.
10 + 5 = 15	I know 10 + 5 equals 15, so 8 + 7 equals 15.

Notice that this thinking process requires three prerequisite foundational facts. Students must know the combinations of 10 (as a missing addend: 8 + ? = 10), the combinations that add up to 7 (and/or the +/- 2 facts), and the 10 + ___ facts. Applying these three pieces mentally is perhaps more challenging and requires more time than we anticipate. If a student is struggling with the Making 10 strategy, figuring out which of these foundational facts groups might need additional support is very important (see Chapter 6 for some assessment tools to help diagnose what students know).

Is this strategy worth the effort? Absolutely! The Making 10 strategy is integrally tied to place value concepts, helping students think about 10 simultaneously as a group of 10 units and as a single group of 10. This strategy can (and should) be extended to multidigit computation. Students who have mastered making 10 might "make 20" to solve 18 + 7 (18 + 2 = 20, 20 + 5 = 25), "make 100" to solve 80 + 70 (80 + 20 = 100, 100 + 50 = 150), and so on. Consider the problem 1,999 + 331. Using the traditional algorithm would be cumbersome, while using a "make 1,000" strategy changes the problem to 2,000 + 330, which can be calculated mentally with greater efficiency. Efficiency is central to fluency; therefore, learning the Making 10 strategy is important for developing not only basic fact fluency but also fluency with addition and subtraction in general.

Quick looks for Making 10. Just as with Near Doubles, carefully arranged double ten frames can be used to encourage students to "invent" the Making 10 strategy. Consider the two images in Figure 3.7. Notice that, in each image, the careful arrangement of the dots facilitates simply moving dots over from the right-hand ten frame to complete the ten frame on the left. Then students can simply add the remaining dots to 10, an easy sum.

The quick look routine of only providing two to three seconds per look facilitates this thinking, as students are motivated to find efficient ways to make sense of the image. Finally, initial work with such images should be followed with connecting the visuals to number sentences and words to describe the strategy. The teacher might write these sentences for the quick look image on the right.

8 + 7 = ?
8 + 2 = 10, and 7 − 2 = 5
10 + 5 = 15, so
8 + 7 = 15

Pretend-a-10. This strategy is not as well known as Making 10, but Baroody and colleagues (2016) indicate that we should be using it more. These researchers call this the Use 10 strategy, which we have adapted as Pretend-a-10 to help students remember the first step and to distinguish the strategy from Making 10. The first step of this strategy is to pretend one of the numbers is 10. You then derive the actual answer by adjusting for this change. Figure 3.8 uses the same numbers from Figure 3.6 to illustrate a student's thinking for Pretend-a-10.

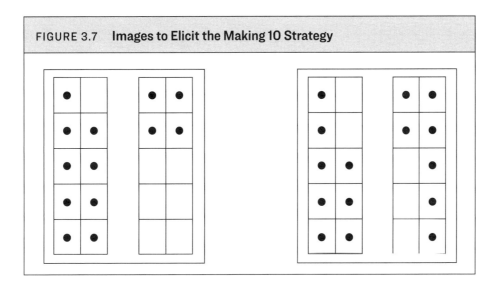

FIGURE 3.7   **Images to Elicit the Making 10 Strategy**

Which foundational facts underlie this strategy? In this case, the student drew on the 10 + ___ facts, combinations of 10 as missing addends (8 + ___ = 10), and, finally, +/- 1 or 2 facts. How does this compare to the foundational facts that are used in Making 10? The main difference is that, in Making 10, a student must know how to decompose one of the addends; in Pretend-a-10 they only decompose the number 10. Baroody and colleagues (2016) found that students who learned this strategy and practiced it while playing games did substantially better than their peers on addition facts involving adding 8s or 9s. It is possible that this occurred because the Pretend-a-10 strategy poses less cognitive challenge than Making 10.

Quick looks such as those featured in Figure 3.7 could also be used to motivate the Pretend-a-10 **strategy**. When students share their thinking, listen for descriptions that involve pretending one of the ten frames was actually full, finding that total, and then removing the imagined dots. For example, the image for 8 + 7 might be solved by thinking 10 + 7 = 17 and then removing the two added dots to get 15. Note that, in this strategy, no dots are moved; imaginary dots are simply added and then taken away. This distinction can be drawn as students explain their strategies to the class.

FIGURE 3.8 Pretend-a-10 Strategy Reasoning	
Mental Process in Symbols	**What Students Might Think or Say as They Solve**
$8 + 7 =$ ___	I am going to pretend the 8 is a 10.
$8^{10} + 7 =$ ___	I know my 10 + ___ facts. This equals 17.
$10 + 7 = 17$	I have to adjust my answer. Eight is 2 away from 10, so I need to take 2 away from 17.
$17 - 2 = 15$	Two less than 17 is 15.

Other Invented Addition Strategies

Although Near Doubles, Making 10, and Pretend-a-10 are derived fact strategies that we believe must receive explicit instruction, there are other strategies that students may invent. For example, because the ten frames also highlight 5 as a benchmark, students might see the 5s and put those 5s together to make a 10 (Figure 3.9).

FIGURE 3.9 Highlight 5 Strategy Reasoning	
Mental Process in Symbols	**What a Student Might Think or Say as They Solve**
$8 + 7 =$ ___?	Both of these numbers are 5 and some more, so the answer is 10 plus those extras.
$5 + 3 + 5 + 2 = ?$	I break 8 into 5 and 3 and 7 into 5 and 2. Then I add the 5s.
$5 + 5 = 10$ $3 + 2 = 5$	The 5s make 10, and then the extras (3 and 2) make another 5.
$10 + 5 = 15$	10 and 5 makes 15, so my answer is 15.

If the strategies students invent reflect the efficiency, accuracy, and appropriateness indicative of fluency, it is important to add them to your class list of reasonable ways to solve problems with basic facts.

Potential Pitfalls

The strategies discussed in this chapter are efficient and highly effective for helping students master any challenging addition combination. In fact, these strategies are so effective that it is difficult to find a textbook for 1st or 2nd grade that doesn't include the Near Doubles and Making 10 strategies (although the names of the strategies may differ). However, there are three common pitfalls that many curricula and teachers make when it comes to introducing derived fact strategies—mistakes that you will want to avoid!

Insufficient mastery of foundational facts. If you teach 1st or 2nd grade, a necessary first step in introducing derived fact strategies is to identify where they appear in your curriculum in relation to the prerequisite foundational facts. It is not uncommon for textbooks to pair the introduction of a derived fact strategy with the foundational facts underlying it. For example, on Monday, a class may study doubles facts, and on Tuesday, they may be introduced to the Near Doubles strategy. But students do not pick up the Near Doubles strategy. Why? Consider the thinking process shared earlier for solving 6 + 7: Start from the easier doubles fact (6 + 6 = 12) and add 1 more to get 13. *This strategy only makes sense if you already know (automatically) that 6 + 6 = 12; otherwise, it is meaningless.* And automaticity with doubles is not going to happen overnight. For this reason, students are unable to make sense of derived fact strategies presented in such quick succession after their related foundational facts. It is therefore necessary for teachers to examine and possibly re-sequence existing lessons to ensure that sufficient time and practice is devoted to mastering foundational facts before the corresponding derived fact strategies are introduced.

Strategies are shown but not really learned. Many textbooks and other resources present derived fact strategies such as Near Doubles or Making 10. These resources (and related instruction) may include visual aids, such as double ten frames, to help show how the strategy works. Yet students are unable to use the strategy on their own. An important question to consider in explicit strategy instruction is *who* is doing the thinking for the strategy? For example, a common illustration for introducing Making 10 is to use arrows to indicate the movement of one or more counters from one ten frame to fill another, as shown in Figure 3.10.

FIGURE 3.10   Illustration of Making 10 Thinking

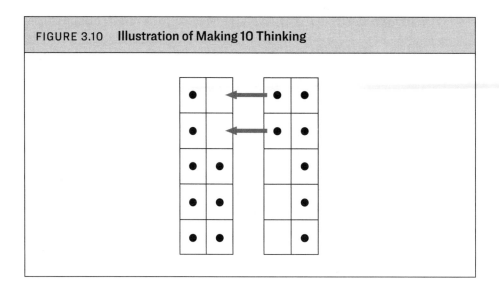

Although this is more helpful than just using words or number sentences, it lacks a critical element of effective strategy development: The students have not developed and internalized the idea of decomposing a number, deciding how to break it apart (decompose it) and how to use their known facts. This decision making is at the heart of fluency. Seeing examples where the decisions have been made may be helpful, but it is insufficient. Students must have opportunities to generate ways to decompose numbers to apply a strategy, like Near Doubles, seeing that they have options. And, they must have opportunities to choose among the strategies for a given fact (e.g., 7 + 8). Students must be encouraged to develop derived fact strategies *with ownership*, using carefully selected and sequenced quick looks, as discussed earlier.

Strategies are not emphasized in practice. Derived fact strategies are grounded in number sense (and the ability to decompose numbers). Students with a strong number sense will employ derived fact strategies without much pushing. Students without a strong number sense, however, may resist moving away from counting to attempt such strategies, particularly if they are quick counters. Thinking through a strategy is harder and requires more time (initially)! This is one of the reasons timed tests and speed games are detrimental to students: Under the pressure of time, students just default to counting rather than slowing down to consider a strategy that would eventually help them become faster and more efficient. Although quick looks are designed to nudge students away from counting, many other forms of practice, including games, do not have a natural safeguard against it. Teachers need to explicitly encourage the use of strategies during game play. This vignette illustrates a common way this might be done as a teacher observes game play.

Garrett: My cards are 4 and 5, so I have … 5, 6, 7—

Teacher (interrupting): Hold on, Garrett. Let's see if we can solve this an easier way. You're trying to solve 4 + 5, right? Can you think of anything that could help you solve this?

Garrett: I can put the big number in my head and count on.

Teacher: Yes, but how about using a helper fact instead? Can you think of any facts that you know that could help you solve 4 + 5?

Garrett: Well, I know 4 + 4 = 8 . . .

Teacher: So how can that help you with 4 + 5?

Garrett: I don't know … I usually just count.

Teacher: I think your idea of using 4 + 4 = 8 is a good one. Let's stick with that. If 4 + 4 = 8, then what would 4 + 5 have to be?

Garrett: It would have to be one more. It would have to be 9.

Teacher: Why?

Garrett: Because 4 is 1 less than 5, so if I start with 4 + 4 = 8, I still have to put that one back. And I know one more than 8 is 9.

Teacher: Let's see if you could use that strategy again, maybe on these two cards (6 and 7)?

As this vignette shows, some students will opt to use counting even if they can apply a strategy. These students need extra encouragement to select and use strategies, even if at first this may be slower. For this reason, it is important to select games that do not have time as a factor in "winning" or "succeeding" when students are still developing strategies. Over time and with explicit instructions to use strategies, students' comfort with how and when to use the strategies will increase. Encouraging strategy use can be facilitated through group discussion of strategies before and after game play or by using journal prompts, such as those featured in Chapter 7.

Games for Derived Addition Fact Strategies

Games provide an important venue for practicing strategies and encourage students to move from Phase 2 to Phase 3 with addition facts. With foundational facts, you may have noticed that we identified games for each type of fact. Here, however, we take the opposite approach and provide games that apply *across derived fact strategies.* The reason for having games that cross strategies is so that students can select and apply an appropriate derived fact strategy. For the example 8 + 7 used to illustrate several strategies in this chapter, a student might use Near Doubles, Making 10, Pretend-a-10, or even Highlight 5s to determine the sum. As long as they are not counting, they are making progress toward mastery. Playing games gives students practice not just in *using* a strategy but also in *choosing* a strategy. That being said, it is still appropriate to play any one of these games and ask students to practice a new strategy they have just learned, requesting they think aloud as they play.

Games 11 and 12 describe two games that are particularly effective for addition fact strategy practice.

GAME 11
LUCKY 13   ● ● ● ●

For two to four players, you need: one deck of numeral cards or playing cards with kings and jacks removed (ace = 1, queen = 0), score card or notebook, pencil, calculators (optional)

How to play: Each player turns over four cards. From their cards, each player picks two cards which, when added together, produce a sum as close to 13 as possible. Then they add these two numbers together, record the sum, and determine how far their total is from 13. (For example, if the two cards add to 11, the score is 2 because 11 is 2 away from 13.) Each player records the difference on a score card or in a notebook. Players discard all their cards, and the dealer gives each player four new cards. Play repeats for five rounds, and then players add their points from each round. The person with the lowest score wins.

Possible variations: Change the lucky number. Use any combination of cards to add to 13. (For example, a player may use all four of their cards.) Change to subtraction, with a lower lucky number (e.g., 3). Change to multiplication, with a greater lucky number, like 24.

GAME 12
SUM WAR

For each pair of players, you need: one deck of numeral cards or playing cards with kings and jacks removed (ace = 1, queen = 0)

How to play: Split the deck so that each player has half of the cards. At the same time, each player turns over two cards and calls out the sum of their numbers. Each player checks their partner's sums. If both are correct, the person with the greater sum wins. If only one player is correct, that player wins. If neither is correct, the cards go to the bottom of each player's deck. The winning player keeps the cards. Play continues until one of the decks is gone or time is called. The player with the most cards wins.

Possible variations: Use only cards 0–5. Use 3 addends (three cards each). Change to subtraction. Find the difference, and the player with the lesser difference wins the cards. Change to multiplication, comparing products instead of sums.

Many familiar games can easily be adapted for practice with basic addition facts. Here are examples of five classic games.

FAMILIAR GAMES ADAPTED FOR BASIC FACTS

Game 13: Bingo

Version 1: You call out addition facts, and students mark the sums. Students can prepare their own bingo boards by writing sums (from a list you provide) in the squares wherever they like.

Version 2: Do the reverse of Version 1. Students write facts from a given set in each square of their board wherever they like. You call out the sums, and students select a fact with that sum.

Game 14: Concentration

Create card pairs with fact expressions (e.g., 8 + 9) and corresponding sums (e.g., 17). This can be quickly done by creating a table with the facts in one column and

**FAMILIAR GAMES ADAPTED
FOR BASIC FACTS**—*(continued)*

corresponding sums in the other, printing the table on cardstock, and cutting out the cells. Place cards facedown in an array. Students turn over two cards, looking for a matching expression and sum. Students keep any matches they find, and the player with the most matches wins. An alternative is to illustrate the expression cards with small ten frames to help students apply strategies they have learned.

Game 15: Dominoes

Create (or find) dominoes that have a fact on one half (e.g., 3 + 9) and the sum for a different fact on the other half (e.g., 9). Give each player the same number of dominoes (about 10). Students take turns finding dominoes they can play by matching an expression with an equivalent expression or corresponding sum.

Game 16: Four in a Row

This partner game is excellent for supporting mastery of fact sets and strategies. Create a 6 × 6 square game board with a sum from 0–18 in each square. Give each partner a pile of counters, each with their own color.

Version 1 (easier): Have students take turns drawing two number cards or playing cards with kings and jacks removed (ace = 1, queen = 0) and covering a square with that sum, continuing until someone gets four in a row.

Version 2 (more strategic): Write the numerals 0–9 underneath the game board. The first player places markers on any two numerals, adds them together, and then places his counter on any square that has that sum. (For example, a player who selects 6 and 9 places a marker on the sum, 15.) The second player then moves only one marker to a different numeral and then places her counter on any untaken square with that sum. Players continue to take turns, trying to build four in a row in their own color (or trying to block their opponent from getting four in a row). The first player to get four in a row wins the game.

Game 17: Old Mascot (Old Maid)

Use cards as described for Concentration. Add one card that has a picture of your school mascot. Play in groups of three to five players. Shuffle and deal all cards. Players go around the circle and take turns drawing cards from the person on their right. If they draw a card that is a match (a fact and its sum), they lay down the pair. Continue until all matches are found and someone is left with the Old Mascot.

Subtraction Derived Fact Strategies

As with addition, students need explicit instruction and significant opportunities to practice subtraction strategies. Without these opportunities, students can depend on Counting Up or Counting Back, which can sometimes be useful but are often inefficient. Think Addition is a very common and effective strategy, one of several that connect to addition. To start thinking about subtraction strategies, examine the 10 subtraction facts shown in Figure 3.11 and sort them into groups based on how students might efficiently solve them.

FIGURE 3.11 Subtraction Facts		
17 – 8	15 – 3	12 – 5
13 – 6	11 – 2	15 – 9
15 – 7	16 – 8	8 – 6
14 – 3	11 – 9	13 – 4

Of course, there are multiple ways to sort these facts. Throughout this section, we will refer back to the subtraction facts you sorted from this table.

Counting Up or Counting Back

Although counting methods are generally not the most efficient, there are exceptions. Perhaps you grouped 11 – 2 and 15 – 3 together, recognizing that both can be solved efficiently by simply counting back from the minuend. Conceptually, this connects to subtraction as "take away." You may have also placed 8 – 6 and 11 – 9 together because both can be efficiently solved by counting up from the subtrahend, or lesser number, until the greater number is reached. Conceptually, this connects to subtraction as "compare," finding the distance (or difference) between two numbers (e.g., how much greater/longer/more is 11 than 9?). One key to developing fluency with subtraction facts is helping students to recognize the distinction between take away and compare situations. Students who always think of subtraction as taking away, especially with facts where the two values are close together (such as 8 – 6), are not using an efficient strategy. A number line can help students contrast these two situations, as illustrated in Figure 3.12. Students can find 14 – 3 by counting back (take away) and agree that is efficient, but when they find 11 – 9, they find that a take-away approach is *not* efficient. Instead, they need to think about the distance between the numbers.

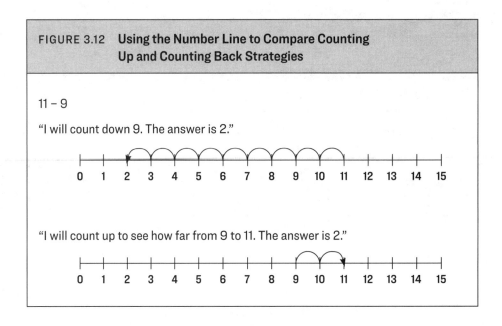

FIGURE 3.12   **Using the Number Line to Compare Counting Up and Counting Back Strategies**

11 – 9

"I will count down 9. The answer is 2."

"I will count up to see how far from 9 to 11. The answer is 2."

Students can sort out just the subtraction facts that fit either the Counting Back or Counting Up strategies. After sorting has been completed, students can discuss when each option is efficient and when it is not. Because take-away situations are far more common, students often need additional practice in thinking about subtraction as comparing. Game 18 can help.

Think Addition

Addition is generally easier than subtraction for many students. Therefore, it is no surprise that many students approach the learning of subtraction facts by thinking of related addition facts. For example, when finding 12 – 5, students may instead think 5 + ? = 12 and rely on their knowledge of addition facts to solve. Notice that this strategy is connected to and advances the Counting Up strategy. Think Addition can also be supported by the number line. When a student uses Think Addition, they are virtually asking, "What is the jump from 5 to 12? Do I know this jump *without having to count?*"

GAME 18
DIFFY DOZEN

● ● ● ●

For each pair of players, you need: two dice or number cubes and 12 counters per player

How to play: Players take turns rolling the dice and finding the difference between the two numbers. The player with the greater difference takes that number of counters from the other player. Continue until a player is unable to give the number of counters required or until 10 rounds have been completed. The player with the most counters wins.

Possible variations: Play with a group of three to five players, passing the dice around the circle. Use 10-sided dice or a deck of cards to include greater differences. (This means that players will need more counters.)

One way to help students see the connection between known addition facts and subtraction facts is to practice generating "fact families," *starting* with the subtraction fact and inviting students to offer the related addition fact:

12 − 5 = 7   5 + 7 = 12
12 − 7 = 5   7 + 5 = 12

An excellent way to practice Think Addition is through the game Salute, which is described below (Bay-Williams & Kling, 2014). You may also wish to provide recording sheets so that students can record the fact families for several rounds as they play, reinforcing the connection between addition and subtraction.

GAME 19

SALUTE

● ● ● ●

For groups of three players, you need: ten frame cards or deck of playing cards with kings and jacks removed (ace = 1, queen = 0)

How to play: Determine which of the three students will be the leader for the first draw. This player takes the deck (facedown) and gives each of the other two players a card. Without looking at the cards, the players hold them on their foreheads facing outward, so the others can see them. The leader says the sum of the two cards. The other two players determine the value of the card on their foreheads, based on hearing the sum and seeing the card on the other player's forehead (one addend). Both players share how they determined their numbers; then the cards are discarded. The player to the right of the leader becomes the leader for the next round. Continue play until the deck is gone.

Possible variations: Use only a select group of cards, such as numbers 1–5. Include a fourth player. The leader now finds the sum of three cards, and the players must determine their cards by finding the difference between the sum of all three and the sum of the other two. Score points by awarding all the cards to the player who answers first with the correct number.

Students may find it particularly useful to apply Think Addition in cases involving the inverse of an addition double, such as $14 - 7$ and $16 - 8$. These may be among the easiest subtraction facts for students to solve, given the relative ease with which students develop automaticity with the related doubles facts. However, students can also apply Think Addition to reverse Near Doubles facts with good success. For example, students may solve $13 - 6$ by thinking of the nearby subtraction fact $12 - 6 = 6$ and reasoning that 13 is one more, so $13 - 6$ is 7. Alternately, they may solve $13 - 6$ by recognizing that when they think addition ($6 + ? = 13$), they are close to the doubles fact $6 + 6 = 12$, just one greater. This means that the missing number must be one greater than 6, or 7. Prompting students to identify nearby "helper facts" can encourage them to see the connection between the subtraction fact they need to find and nearby doubles facts that may help them.

Using 10 as a Benchmark

Students may also make use of their knowledge of combinations of 10 and 10 + __ facts to help them find subtraction facts. This often occurs when the minuend is a teen number and the subtrahend is slightly less than 10, such as 15 − 9 or 17 − 8. There are a variety of ways students might reason through these facts, with a common theme of using 10 as a benchmark.

The first two strategies in this group, Down over 10 and Up over 10, are virtually Counting Back and Counting Up strategies. Instead of counting by ones, however, students start at one number, jump to the 10, and then jump to the other number to find the difference. There are two distinct situations (take-away and compare) that may be used.

Down over 10. Students using this reasoning strategy can go "down to 10" in one of two ways (Figure 3.13).

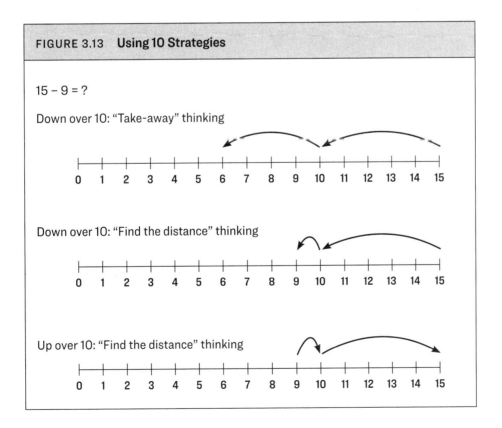

FIGURE 3.13   Using 10 Strategies

15 − 9 = ?

Down over 10: "Take-away" thinking

Down over 10: "Find the distance" thinking

Up over 10: "Find the distance" thinking

In take-away thinking, a student finds 15 – 9 by asking, "How much will I have left after taking away 9?" He then jumps from 15 to 10, a jump of 5, and jumps 4 more to reach 6. Taking away 9 leaves 6, so 15 – 9 = 6. In compare thinking, the student finds 15 – 9 by asking, "How far apart are 15 and 9?" He then jumps from 15 to 10, a jump of 5, and jumps down one more to reach 9. Since the total number of jumps is 6, the numbers are 6 apart. Thus, 15 – 9 = 6.

Up over 10. Here the student uses compare thinking. The student finds 15 – 9 by starting with 9 and counting up 1 to get to 10. Then he counts up 5 more to get to 15. Since the total number of jumps was 6, 15 – 9 = 6.

An important implication here is that story problems need to include contexts that motivate a compare interpretation (e.g., how much taller is the 15-inch flower than the 9-inch flower?). Too many subtraction stories use a take-away situation, causing students to struggle with understanding subtraction as a difference or distance.

Take from 10. This is a third way to use 10. It takes advantage of students' knowledge of the combinations of 10, as it only involves subtraction from 10. Figure 3.14 is an illustration of the Take from 10 strategy for 15 – 8.

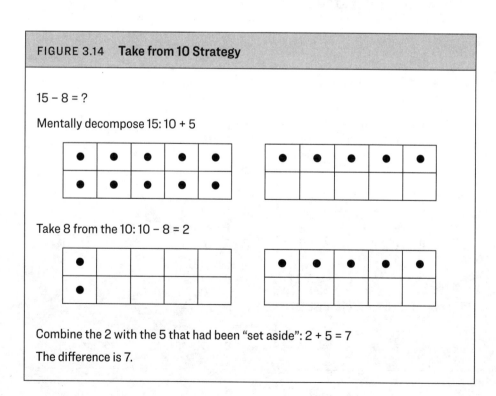

FIGURE 3.14   **Take from 10 Strategy**

15 – 8 = ?

Mentally decompose 15: 10 + 5

Take 8 from the 10: 10 – 8 = 2

Combine the 2 with the 5 that had been "set aside": 2 + 5 = 7

The difference is 7.

When we have used this strategy with students, some are very excited at how "easy" it is and ask, "Will this always work?" Using counting cubes, base ten blocks, or ten frames, students can convince themselves that indeed it does.

The Using 10 strategies are important to learn and understand, not just to become fluent with basic facts, but to become fluent with larger subtraction problems. For example, Take from 10 could be applied to 43 – 15, subtracting 40 – 15 to equal 25 and adding the three back on to equal 28. Problems like 208 – 195 are fitting for a compare interpretation, and students can use a Counting Up strategy to get 13 as the difference between these two numbers (a much more efficient strategy than applying the standard algorithm for subtraction!).

Games for Developing Fluency with Subtraction Facts

Just as with addition facts, students need to practice subtraction fact strategies to develop fluency. However, your goal for learning subtraction facts may be different than your goal for addition. In many states, the expectation for addition facts is automaticity by the end of grade 2; however, with subtraction facts, the expectation is only fluency. Therefore, although students should develop flexibility, accuracy, efficiency, and appropriate strategy use with subtraction, subtraction facts do not need to be answered within three seconds. As with addition, you must be explicit in encouraging students to use strategies as they play games, following up by talking to students about their strategy choices. Because subtraction practice is generally underdone in classrooms, we have provided several excellent games for subtraction and for both operations in this section and the next. Games 20 and 21 will be helpful in encouraging fluency with subtraction, and many of the games previously discussed can be adapted to focus on subtraction (see the possible variations for each game).

Using Games to Achieve Mastery

This chapter contains games that encourage students to choose derived fact strategies for addition, as well as games that focus on specific subtraction strategies. Mastery of the addition facts within 10 and related subtraction facts requires intensive and extensive opportunities to practice the strategies. We close with three fun strategy games that involve a mixture of addition and subtraction. These games, along with Salute (Game 19) are excellent for ongoing practice and summer take-home activities to ensure that students are practicing strategies and maintaining mastery.

Notice that Games 22 and 23 focus on facts within 10 but can be adapted to within 20. Game 24 offers significant practice with adding in the teens.

GAME 20

TARGET DIFFERENCE   ● ● ● ●

For each group of three to four players, you need: deck of cards with kings and jacks removed (ace = 1, queen = 0), one die

How to play: One student deals eight cards to each player, which they place, faceup, in front of them. Another student rolls the die. The number rolled is the target difference. For example, if a 2 is rolled, the students try to find two cards that have a difference of 2, such as 5 and 3. If they have cards with that difference, they remove them. (They may only remove one pair on each turn.) Repeat, taking turns rolling the die. The goal is to be the first player with no cards left.

Possible variations: Have students show on a number line that their cards have a distance/difference equal to the target. Allow students to use more than two cards to create an expression equal to the target.

Summary

Ensuring that students have automaticity with these strategies may be the most important investment you make. Strategy use is not just a mechanism for reaching addition fact mastery; it is a mechanism for increased mathematics achievement *in general* (Jordan, Kaplan, Locuniak, & Ramineni, 2007; Jordan, Kaplan, Ramineni, & Locuniak, 2009; Vasilyeva, Laski, & Shen, 2015). For example, fluency with addition fact strategies predict success with two-digit addition problems (Vasilyeva et al., 2015). These researchers advocate for an increased focus on explicit strategy instruction in the early grades. Given the importance of basic fact fluency for future mathematics learning, helping all students reach fluency and mastery (automaticity) with their addition facts and fluency with their subtraction facts is crucial.

Although it is likely that no parent, teacher, or textbook author would disagree with this need, some textbooks may not provide sufficient instructional strategies and experiences to ensure fluency and mastery/automaticity. This chapter's derived fact strategies, coupled with suggestions of potential pitfalls to avoid, are intended to support and expand existing curriculum materials to create a coherent, effective learning progression for all addition and subtraction facts. Add in frequent, meaning-ful practice with the games in this chapter and effective assessment strategies (see Chapter 7), and you have a recipe for success!

GAME 21
SUBTRACTION STACKS   ● ● ● ●

For each group of two to four players, you need: counters (10 per player), two dice, Subtraction Stacks card for each player (or similar sketch in a notebook)

How to play: Each player counts out 10 counters and places them on their Subtraction Stacks card wherever they want, stacking them on the numbers.

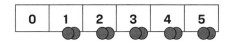

Players take turns rolling both dice and finding the difference between the two num-bers. If the difference is 2, for example, the student removes a counter from the 2 stack. If the player has no counters on that stack, nothing is removed. The player who removes all his or her counters first is the winner.

Possible variations: Extend Subtraction Stacks card to 9 or 11, using 12- or 10-sided dice and giving more counters to each player. Use more counters.

GAME 22

AROUND THE HOUSE

● ● ● ●

For each group of two to three players, you need: three dice, one piece of paper and pencil per player

How to play: Each player draws a "house" and numbers it as shown.

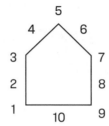

Players number their papers from 1 to 10 to record each expression they find. Players take turns rolling all three dice. They can use just two or all three of the numbers to try to make an expression equal to 1. If they can do this, they mark off the 1 outside the "house." Without rerolling, the player tries to make an expression equal to 2, then 3, and so on. The player's turn is over when an expression cannot be made with the three numbers showing. Play goes to the next person, who re-rolls the dice and repeats the process. The first person who crosses out all the numbers around his "house," in order, is the winner.

Possible variations: Use 10-sided dice and include numbers through 20. Allow students to mark off numbers in any order, instead of moving sequentially. Draw a softball or baseball diamond instead and mark off all the positions with numbers. The player who is the first to "hit" to each of the positions on the field wins.

GAME 23

DIRTY DOZEN

● ● ● ●

For each group of two to four players, you need: two dice, 20 counters for each player, a bowl to hold the counters

How to play: To start the game, everyone puts two counters in the bowl. Players give and take counters from the bowl based on these rules (the player rolling is required to always say out loud the sum rolled before any additional action is taken):

- If you roll a sum that is less than 10 (except 2), find the distance to 10. Put that number of counters in the bowl.
- If you roll a sum of 10 or more, take all the counters in the bowl.
- If you roll "snake eyes" (two 1s), all the other players must put two counters in the bowl.

Players take turns rolling the dice and take or give counters based on the rules. The last player with counters wins the game.

Possible variations: There are many—be creative! For example, to emphasize doubles, you could add the rule, "If you roll doubles, the other players must put two counters into the bowl."

GAME 24

FIRST TO 20   ● ● ● ●

For each group of two to four players, you need: one die, one piece of paper and pencil per player

How to play: The goal of this game is to make it to 20—exactly. On the first turn, players roll the die and write down their first number on their papers. On each subsequent turn, players roll the die and add the number to their previous rolls. If a roll will take them over 20, they must subtract the number rolled. The game ends when one player has an exact score of 20. A recording table can be very helpful in keeping track.

Roll	6	5	3	5	4									
Total	6	11	14	19	15									

↑
(must subtract 4 because 19 + 4 is greater than 20)

Possible variations: Start at 20 and count down to 0. Change game to First to 30. Use 10-sided dice. Use two dice and change the game to First to 100.

4

Foundational Multiplication and Division Facts

Reflecting back on the way in which you learned multiplication facts, it is likely that it involved a process of memorizing and then testing the 0s facts (0 × 0, 0 × 1, etc.), then the 1s facts, the 2s facts, and so on. Although this approach is still common today, introducing facts in sequential order (0s, 1s, 2s, etc.) is inconsistent with research recommendations (Heege, 1985; Kamii & Anderson, 2003; National Research Council, 2001; Thornton, 1978). For example, 10s facts are generally easier to master than most other multiplication facts, yet if the facts were taught in the traditional order, they would be the last to be introduced! Instead, ordering fact learning by ease of mastery, just as with addition and subtraction, is more helpful for a strategies-based approach. This progression is illustrated in Figure 4.1.

Learning foundational multiplication facts first is critical, both when encountering them for the first time and when remediation is needed with older students. This chapter will familiarize you with the various meanings of multiplication and division as well as ways to introduce and practice foundational facts. As we share in each chapter, this chapter connects to the fundamentals of basic fact fluency in these ways.

1. **Mastery must focus on fluency.** Through making connections to addition, and the use of arrays, this chapter focuses on ways to reach mastery through fluency for foundational facts.

2. **Fluency develops in three phases.** Multiplication quick looks and games are explored to help students move from Phase 1 (counting) to Phase 3 (mastery) with foundational facts.

3. **Foundational facts must precede derived facts.** For students to be able to apply strategies fluently (particularly for greater products), they must have mastered foundational facts.

4. **Timed tests do not assess fluency.** Many students can quickly skip count to determine foundational facts such as 10s and 5s, and if they don't eventually move beyond this, they won't achieve mastery. Thus, it is critical to choose assessments that allow you to see what approach they are using, and timed tests do not do this.

5. **Students need substantial and enjoyable practice.** This is certainly true for mastering the foundational facts for multiplication. Games are provided for each foundational fact set, as well as for mixed fact sets.

FIGURE 4.1   **Multiplication: Foundational Facts**

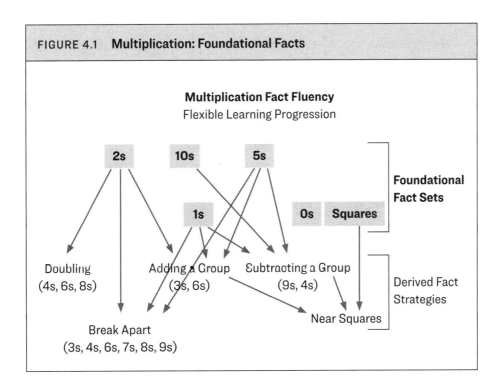

Multiplication: More Than Repeated Addition

It is not a coincidence that many students find it harder to master multiplication facts than addition facts. Simply put, multiplication is a much more difficult operation to understand. Think for a moment about the meaning of each number in each of these basic facts:

$$6 + 5 = ?$$
$$6 \times 5 = ?$$

In the operation of addition, the two addends generally play the same role; both contribute to the overall sum in essentially the same way. For 6 + 5, we are simply combining 6 items with 5 items to make a total of 11 items. In contrast, in multiplication, the two factors have different roles. One factor tells the number of groups, whereas the other factor tells the amount in each group. For example, 6 × 5 means 6 groups, each of which has 5 items in it, for a total of 30 items. For this reason, multiplication is a more challenging operation. However, as with addition and subtraction, this challenge is eased by setting problems in context.

Storytelling

Story problems need to be at the *beginning* of working with multiplication and division, not the end. As stated in Chapter 2, stories connect to students' prior knowledge, build conceptual understanding, and provide concrete context in which to understand the abstract concept and symbols for multiplication and division. The key is to use contexts that make sense to students and have tools available for modeling the problem. For example, students can use modeling to make sense of story problems like this one.

> Anna is making bags for her birthday party guests. She has 6 bags and wants to put 5 treats in each bag. How many treats will Anna need in all?

By using objects, acting, or drawing, students can create models, such as the one shown in Figure 4.2, to help them organize and solve the story.

The way in which a story is told matters. To understand this better, please read these stories, all of which involve either multiplication or division. How would you represent each story?

- Samantha has 2 boxes of crayons. There are 8 crayons in each box. How many crayons does she have in all?

- Our class has 15 chairs. We need to make rows with 3 chairs in each row. How many rows will we make?
- Our classroom has 8 small groups. Each group needs a tray of crayons. We have 80 crayons to share. How many crayons will each group get?
- Gavin lays out his baseball cards in 5 rows. Each row has 10 cards. How many baseball cards does Gavin have?

Some of these situations might be represented using drawings of equal groups (similar to Figure 4.2), while others inspire array representations. Both types of situations are important because students will use both equal group and array models to apply strategies for multiplication facts. There are more multiplication situations beyond equal groups and arrays, but these two are accessible at a younger age and thus lend themselves more to fact fluency, which is why they are the only ones addressed in this book.

FIGURE 4.2   A Student's Solution to the Party Bag Problem

Equal Groups

To reinforce the concept of multiplication, teach students to read "6 × 5" as "6 *groups of* 5." Such language reinforces the idea that the numbers play different roles (6 groups, 5 items in each group). This is particularly important as students attempt to derive unknown multiplication facts. Recall the two facts mentioned at the beginning of this section (6 + 5 and 6 × 5). To solve 6 + 5 = ?, many students will start with the foundational fact 5 + 5 = 10 and then simply add 1 more to make 11. Is there an analogous strategy for 6 × 5? Starting from 5 × 5 = 25 is reasonable, but adding 1 more to equal 26 is incorrect. This is because we aren't decomposing 6 into 5 and 1; instead we must think of 5 *groups* of 5 and 1 *group* of 5. Therefore, 1 group of 5 needs to be added on to 25, giving a total of 30. Developing fluency will require the flexibility to manipulate the number of groups or the number in each group when solving problems. Thus, future success with multiplication depends upon first understanding what the operation actually means.

Understanding multiplication as equal groups naturally segues to its inverse operation, division. In division, we know the total, or product, and are finding either the number of groups or the amount in each group (i.e., one of the factors). In the first case, we know the amount in each group and are trying to determine the number of groups. This type of division is often called *measurement division*. The second type, *partitive division*, occurs when the number of groups is known and the amount in each group is unknown. Figure 4.3 shows these three story types, along with a sample student illustration for each.

FIGURE 4.3   **Equal Group Stories for Multiplication and Division**

Multiplication	**Measurement Division**	**Partitive Division**
Malik has 3 bags of cookies. In each bag, he has 4 cookies. How many cookies does Malik have in all?	Malik has 12 cookies to separate into bags. He wants to put 4 cookies in each bag. How many bags can he fill?	Malik has 12 cookies to place into 3 bags. Each bag must have the same amount. How many cookies should Malik place in each bag?

(The student draws 12 cookies and then circles each group of 4.)

(The student draws 3 bags and then draws 4 cookies in each bag.)

(The student draws 12 cookies and 3 bags, puts 1 cookie in each bag, and repeats until all the cookies are gone.)

It is not necessary for students to label the different types of multiplication and division problems, but they do need exposure and practice with story problems of each type. These experiences support students' conceptual understanding of division as measurement and as sharing, facilitating their progress toward division fact fluency. When just solving basic division facts, students may or may not create a context, but they will likely utilize the relationship between multiplication and division. In fact, the primary strategy for approaching division facts is thinking of related missing factor problems (Kouba 1989; Mulligan & Mitchelmore, 1997; National Research Council, 2001; Thornton, 1978). For example, given the problem 56 ÷ 7 = ?, students instead think ? × 7 = 56 (how many groups of 7 equal 56?). Ideas for practicing this skill will be explored in Chapter 5.

Arrays

Arrays are a variation of equal groups. In this case, the group is arranged in rows, and the amount in each group corresponds to the number of columns produced in the arrangement. The rectangular row-and-column formation produced, shown in Figure 4.4, is called an *array*.

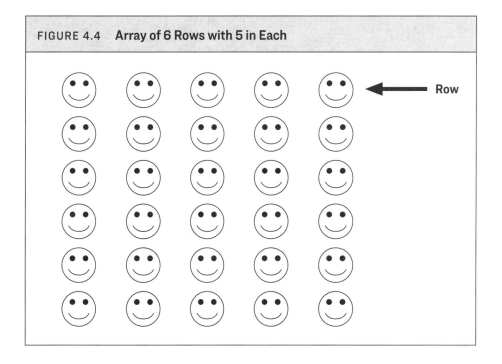

FIGURE 4.4   **Array of 6 Rows with 5 in Each**

Row

Because there are 6 rows (groups) with 5 items in each row (group) for a total of 30 items, this array could be used to model the multiplication fact 6 × 5 = 30. Arrays will naturally emerge when students are presented with contexts involving rectangular arrangements, as in this story problem:

Ms. Carr is arranging her classroom for the first day of school. She has 6 rows of desks, with 5 desks in each row. How many desks are there in all?

Arrays are particularly useful representations of multiplication for several reasons.

- **Arrays can be quickly generated.** Simple circles or Xs can be drawn to represent each item.
- **Arrays help students make sense of the commutative property of multiplication.** Simply turning the array 90 degrees shows that, although the factors are now in reverse order, the product remains the same (see Figure 4.5).

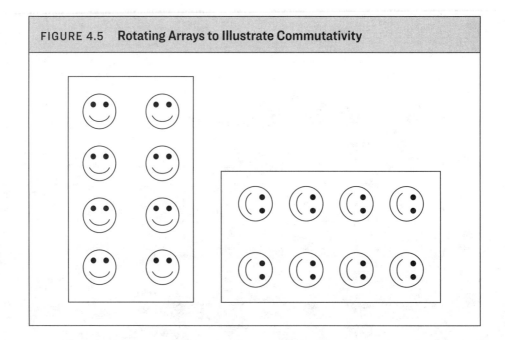

FIGURE 4.5   **Rotating Arrays to Illustrate Commutativity**

- **Arrays can be used to strengthen students' understanding of division as a missing factor.** For example, you can cover some of the rows on the illustration on the left in Figure 4.5 and ask, "How many rows are there if there are

8 smileys in all?" This can help students see how ? × 2 = 8 can be connected to 8 ÷ 2 = ?.

- **Arrays lend themselves to illustrating break-apart strategies.** As shown in Figure 4.6, students can draw a line (or use a marker, such as a piece of uncooked spaghetti) between two of the rows to see that 6 × 5 is equal to 5 rows of 5 and one more row of 5. (This idea of "break apart" to derive unknown facts will be developed in Chapter 5.)

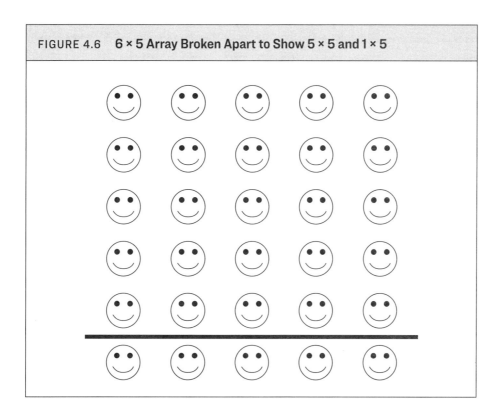

FIGURE 4.6   **6 × 5 Array Broken Apart to Show 5 × 5 and 1 × 5**

- **Arrays provide a natural foundation for work in later grades.** Arrays can be used to model many other concepts, including multidigit multiplication and the area of a rectangle.

Quick Looks

As demonstrated in Chapter 2, quick looks are commonly used to help students decompose numbers within 20. However, quick looks can also be quite effective in helping students see relationships that help them learn the foundational multiplication facts.

Images of dots arranged into equal groups or arrays can be used for practicing multiplication facts with lesser factors. Pages 15–16 outline an effective process for using quick looks: Each image is shown for two to three seconds, hidden, and then shown again for a second look. Then students describe both how many they saw and how they saw it. Having multiple students share their thinking ensures a variety of strategies will emerge, as shown in Figure 4.7.

FIGURE 4.7   **Examples of Multiplication Quick Looks**

Quick Look Image	Sample Student Responses
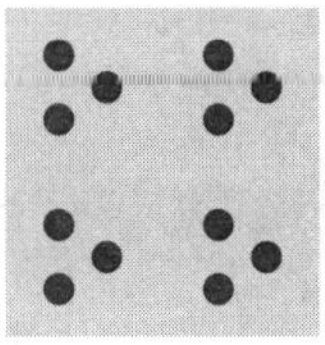	• "I know 3 + 3 = 6 and 6 + 6 = 12, so there are 12 dots." • "I skip counted: 3, 6, 9, 12." • "I know 3 groups of 3 make 9, so I added one more group of 3 to make 12." • "I saw 4 groups of 3, and I just know that makes 12."
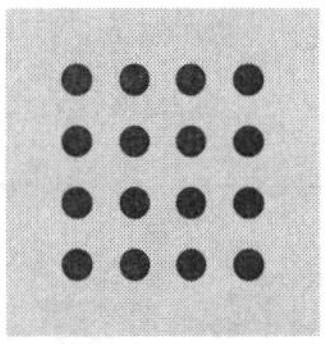	• "I skip counted by 4s because there are 4 in each row." • "I used doubling. I know 4 + 4 = 8, which takes care of the top part. Then I doubled 8 to get 16." • "I split it down the middle into two 4 by 2 arrays. I know each array has 8 dots. 8 + 8 = 16, so there are 16 total dots."

Informal exposure to and practice with story problems and quick looks are important first steps toward multiplication fact fluency. Games and activities can also support an understanding of multiplication, helping students to build on their understanding of addition.

GAME 25
STICKER BOOK PATTERNS

For each group of four players, you need: 72 counters, 1 die, 2 sheets of paper

How to play: Students work in teams of two with one sheet of paper and 36 counters, or "stickers," per team. Students pretend they are arranging stickers on a page. Team 1 places stickers in equal groups, using the first roll of the die to tell the number of groups and the second to tell the number in each group. Team 2 places stickers in arrays, using the first roll to tell the number of rows and the second to tell the number of columns. After both teams have created their "sticker pages" and determined the number of stickers needed, they compare their answers. On the next play, teams exchange tasks, with Team 1 creating arrays and Team 2 creating equal groups. After the game is finished, discuss how the sticker patterns compare.

Possible variations (to apply the commutative property of multiplication): Have both teams work on the same task (e.g., equal groups). Roll two dice of different colors and have each team use the numbers in the opposite way. For example, Team 1 could use the roll of a red die to tell number of groups, while Team 2 uses it to tell the amount in each group. Have both teams work on the same task (e.g., arrays). Roll two dice that are the same, but let the students decide which number will indicate the number of columns and which will indicate the number of rows.

A Progression for Foundational Multiplication Facts

Once an understanding of multiplication as equal groups or arrays has been firmly established, students can begin more formal work learning multiplication facts. In general, the easiest group of facts for students to learn are the 2s facts, followed by the 10s and 5s (Heege, 1985; Kamii & Anderson, 2003; Watanabe, 2003). These first sets of facts can be introduced as early as the end of 2nd grade. As their understanding of multiplication deepens, students can next begin learning the 1s and 0s facts. Finally, multiplication squares (2 × 2, 3 × 3, etc.) make up the last group of foundational multiplication facts. All the foundational facts are highlighted in Figure 4.8. Notice how few derived facts remain—a powerful illustration of how a focus on foundational facts can greatly support mastering all the multiplication facts.

×	0	1	2	3	4	5	6	7	8	9	10
FIGURE 4.8			**Multiplication Table with Foundational Facts Highlighted**								
0	0	0	0	0	0	0	0	0	0	0	0
1	0	1	2	3	4	5	6	7	8	9	10
2	0	2	4	6	8	10	12	14	16	18	20
3	0	3	6	9	12	15	18	21	24	27	30
4	0	4	8	12	16	20	24	28	32	36	40
5	0	5	10	15	20	25	30	35	40	45	50
6	0	6	12	18	24	30	36	42	48	54	60
7	0	7	14	21	28	35	42	49	56	63	70
8	0	8	16	24	32	40	48	56	64	72	80
9	0	9	18	27	36	45	54	63	72	81	90
10	0	10	20	30	40	50	60	70	80	90	100

Each group of foundational facts provides support for one or more groups of derived multiplication facts. Thus, it is important to master all of the foundational facts first and then target the remaining facts. This progression applies not only when students initially learn multiplication but also for remediation with older students.

Beginning Facts: 2s, 10s, and 5s

Without realizing it, many students enter 3rd grade having already mastered at least one group of multiplication facts (2s) with significant experience with 10s (place value) and 5s (skip counting). Therefore, these three fact sets form the first set of foundational facts.

Notice how these three sets of facts, especially the 2s and 5s, are utilized in almost every derived fact strategy. *We cannot overemphasize how important it is to have automaticity with these sets of facts before moving to derived fact strategies.*

Experiences with addition doubles (1 + 1, 2 + 2, etc.) in the early grades not only develops addition and subtraction fact fluency but also results in an added benefit— fluency with the 2s facts in multiplication. Helping students realize that 2 × 6, for example, is the same as the addition double 6 + 6 is generally all that is needed to develop automaticity with the 2s facts. Students can make this connection as they model and solve a collection of story problems involving 2s facts.

- Students are lined up in 2 lines for lunch. There are 10 students in each line. How many students are there in all?
- There are 6 pencils in each pack. You have 2 packs of pencils. How many pencils do you have in all?
- Suppose you have 2 rows of tomato plants with 8 plants in each row. How many plants do you have in all?

Ask that students include an illustration and both addition and multiplication equations to match the story. As students share their solutions with the rest of the class, encourage them to look for patterns in the equations, that is, each time they multiplied by 2, the corresponding addition number sentence was a doubles fact. Students are thus able to generalize that, whenever they multiply by 2, they can think of the corresponding addition double.

Rather than use doubles, students may prefer to rely on skip counting by 2s. Sometimes the wording of a story may lend to skip counting (e.g., 10 lines with 2 students in each line). Although this initially builds on prior knowledge, skip counting is a Phase 1 strategy, and students must have experiences that move them beyond counting. Further experiences with story problems and quick looks can help students to see ? × 2 and 2 × ? as doubles. Games with arrays can also support this understanding. The game On the Double is a good way to practice the 2s facts.

The games from Chapter 2 that focus on doubles can also be adapted for multiplication. Ask students to say or write the multiplication expression instead of (or in addition to) the addition expression.

Like 2s, students tend to learn the 10s relatively quickly because of their prior experiences with place value and hundreds charts. When introducing 10s facts, help students to see the connections among these statements: 3 10s, 3 groups of 10, and 3 × 10. Dimes are a natural context for practicing 10s facts.

Many students find the 5s facts to be more challenging than 2s or 10s, and, as a result, become stuck in the habit of skip counting (Phase 1). Although students may be able to skip count quickly, this is not efficient and does not demonstrate the automaticity that is needed for 5s to be used for derived fact strategies. One way to help is with quick looks that facilitate students seeing how 5s facts are related to 10s facts, as illustrated in Figure 4.9.

GAME 26
ON THE DOUBLE

● ● ● ●

For two to four players, you need: 10-sided die or deck of playing cards with face cards removed (ace = 1), 15 counters per student, 1 On the Double game board for each student

2	4	6	8	10	12	14	16	18	20

How to play: Students place all their counters over different spaces on the game board. (For example, if they think an 8 will occur most often, they may place more counters above the 8. Once counters have been placed, they cannot be moved to a different location. Players take turns rolling the die, doubling the number, saying the corresponding multiplication fact aloud (e.g., "2 times 4 equals 8"), and removing a counter from that space on the board. If they do not have a counter on that number, no counter is removed. The first student to remove all their counters wins the game.

Possible variations: Use the game for other facts, naming it Triple It (for multiplying by 3) or Quadruple (for multiplying by 4). If using playing cards, include kings as wild cards.

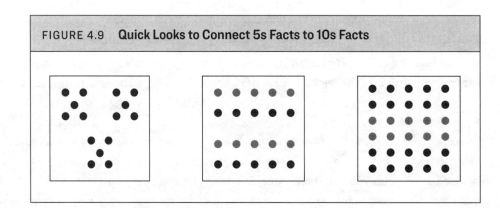

FIGURE 4.9   **Quick Looks to Connect 5s Facts to 10s Facts**

As students share how they see the quick looks, they might see the first one as 3 × 5 or as 10 and 5 more. The second quick look might be seen as 4 × 5 or as 2 × 10, and the third one might be seen as 6 × 5 or as 3 × 10. This pattern can be explored so that students come to see 6 fives as 3 10s, 8 5s as 4 10s, and so on. In effect, students are pairing up the fives to make a 10. This can also be approached through the context of money. Students can exchange groups of nickels for dimes, recording equations for each related set and observing the patterns involved. For example, 6 nickels can be exchanged for 3 dimes (6 × 5 = 30, 3 × 10 = 30), 10 nickels can be exchanged for 5 dimes (10 × 5 = 50, 5 × 10 = 50), and so on. Finally, you can provide students with related 10s and 5s facts and ask them to create their own arrays. The problem sets shown below provide an opportunity to discuss the relationship between these facts.

Changing Number in the Group

10 × 3	5 × 3
10 × 7	5 × 7
10 × 5	5 × 5

Changing Group Size

4 × 10	4 × 5
6 × 10	6 × 5
8 × 10	8 × 5

Recall the importance of mental images in learning the facts. After exploring a few quick looks, money contexts, and student-made arrays, ask students to picture an image of a 5s fact to help them find the product *without* skip counting.

Many games can be adapted to practice 2s, 5s, and 10s. Trios (an adaptation of Four in a Row) is explained for 5s in Game 27 but can be adapted to 2s or 10s as well. Before beginning a game, explicitly coach students to use strategies, rather than skip count, as they play.

Notice that Trios involves related division facts. A student who sees a 20 in one square wonders what is needed to get that square, which is the same as asking, "What times 5 equals 20?" or "Five times what equals 20?"

Once strategies are established for the 2s, 10s, and 5s, sufficient practice is needed to promote mastery of all three of these important foundational fact sets, as in the game Capture 5 First.

GAME 27

TRIOS

● ● ● ●

For two players, you need: 10-sided die or deck of playing cards with face cards removed (ace = 1), one 5 × 5 game board with a multiple of 5 in each square, 15 counters in one color and 15 in another color (or two colors of markers, if the game board is laminated)

How to play: Players take turns rolling the die (or choosing a card), multiplying the number by 5, and placing a counter of their chosen color on any square with that product. The object is to cover three spaces in a row (horizontally, vertically, or diagonally) with the same color. Each successful trio earns the player five points. The person with the highest score wins. New trios can intersect but only by one number.

Possible variations: Change the size of the game board. Change the multiples on the board for other fact sets. Change to Four in a Row.

GAME 28

CAPTURE 5 FIRST

● ● ● ●

For two players, you need: deck of playing cards with face cards removed (ace = 1), 9 index cards per player

How to play: Players prepare for the game by writing 2 on three of their index cards, 5 on three cards, and 10 on the remaining three. Each player takes a card from the deck without showing it to the other student. They then pair this card with an index card in their hand, hoping to create the greater product. Both students reveal their cards, and the player with the greater product receives a point. The playing cards and index cards are both discarded, and play continues. The first player to score five points wins the game.

Possible variation: Change the index cards to other factors to practice different fact sets.

Special Properties Fact Sets: 1s and 0s

Teachers are often surprised at the suggestion that they delay teaching the 1s and 0s multiplication facts. After all, even young students can be taught to recite "anything times one is that number" and "zero times anything is zero," so why the delay? There are several important reasons. First, students commonly confuse the zero property and the identity for multiplication with each other, as well as with the +0 and +1 facts. Second, if students don't understand that 1 times a number means *one group* of that number, they won't be able to use the idea to develop derived fact strategies. Therefore, efforts to teach these facts must focus on developing a conceptual understanding of their meaning. Understanding what happens when we multiply by 1 or 0 is a bit more challenging than understanding multiplying by 2, 5, or 10. Learning these facts must be approached through story problems so that meaning and mastery are developed simultaneously and meaningless rules (such as "zero times anything is zero") are avoided.

To explore 1s facts, students should create representations for familiar contexts, such as packs of gum or forests of trees. A pack of gum containing five sticks can be thought of as "1 group of 5" and written as 1 × 5. Similarly, students can sketch 1 row with 5 trees (1 × 5), or 5 rows with 1 tree in each row (5 × 1). When students see 1 × __ or __ × 1 and can picture 1 row or one group, they will be able to understand *and* remember that the product is the same as the other factor.

Similarly, meaning must be developed for multiplying by zero. What does 0 × 4 mean? Using what we know about multiplication, we can interpret this as "0 groups of 4." Add a context, like four boxes of cereal. If I have zero boxes (groups), I have zero cereal, so the answer of 0 makes sense. What does 4 × 0 mean? Using the cereal boxes, they could be empty boxes (0 in each). Having four empty boxes still leads to 0 cereal. One reason students struggle with 0 facts is they just don't show up enough in story problems or in games. All the games already given in this chapter can be played by adding in a zero card (one of the face cards), and 10-sided dice have a 0.

Multiplication Squares

The final group of foundational multiplication facts are the squares, or products of numbers with themselves (0 × 0, 1 × 1, 2 × 2, etc.). These facts generally are not as readily mastered as the addition doubles, but most students will quickly learn some subset of the squares (Heege, 1985; Thornton, 1978). The name of this group of facts can be very naturally developed when students build arrays where the factors are the same and observe the pattern formed, as illustrated in Figure 4.10.

GAME 29

HOW LOW CAN YOU GO?   ● ● ● ●

For three to four players, you need: a deck of cards with numbers 0–5, 10 (ace = 1, queen = 0, all other face cards and 6, 7, 8, 9 removed)

How to play: The goal is for each player to have three pairs of cards with the lowest overall score. Deal six cards to each player. Place the rest of the deck facedown, with one card turned faceup. Players can pair up their cards however they like to get the lowest products possible. On their turn, a player can take the faceup card or draw from the deck. They discard one of their own cards, faceup (or they can discard the card that they drew). The next player can select from what was discarded or pick from the deck. After three rounds, players lay their cards down to show how low they can go. For example, a player who ended up with 0, 1, 3, 4, 5, 10, can pair her cards this way: 0 × 10, 5 × 1, and 3 × 4. Her score is 17.

Possible variations: Play with all cards 0–10. Deal fewer cards per player. Play for more rounds or play until the music stops (like musical chairs). Include some twists, like when someone discards a "crazy 8," each player gets to draw a card from the person on their right, starting with the person who discarded the 8.

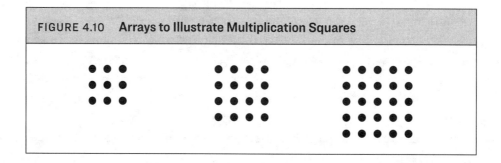

FIGURE 4.10   **Arrays to Illustrate Multiplication Squares**

One reason the multiplication squares are included in this section on foundational facts is their proximity to many of the more challenging multiplication facts. For example, many students in 4th grade and beyond struggle with facts like 7 × 8. However, if they know the multiplication squares, they can start from 7 × 7 or 8 × 8 and derive the answer. An engaging way to practice multiplication squares is through the game Squares Bingo.

GAME 30
SQUARES BINGO

● ● ● ●

For each player, you need: blank 5 × 5 bingo board, bingo chips or counters, deck of playing cards for the teacher with kings and jacks removed (ace = 1, queen = 0)

How to play: Before beginning the game, the teacher posts a list of the square products: 0, 1, 4, 9, 16, 25, 36, 49, 64, 81, and 100. Students copy these numbers into their game boards. (Some numbers will be repeated, and not all numbers must be used.) Then the teacher (or designated leader) draws a card from the deck. Students find the square of that number and cover it on their bingo boards. Only one space can be covered, and chips cannot be moved once they have been placed. The first student to get five in a row (horizontally, diagonally, or vertically) wins the game.

Possible variations: Use the game for other fact groups (except 0s) by changing the products on the game boards. Use a 4 × 4 bingo board.

Notice that with Squares Bingo, the products are on students' game boards. This provides a great opportunity to connect to division as a missing factor. As students near a bingo, ask them to share what equations they are seeking for their products. They may even plead for a specific card: "I only need to cover 64, so please turn over an 8!"

Combined Foundational Facts

Before moving to other multiplication (and related division) facts, it is critical that students know the foundational facts discussed in this chapter. Activities and games can focus on just 2s, 5s, 10s, 1s, 0s, or some combination of these. For example, stories and activities with coins can include 10s (dimes), 5s (nickels), 1s (pennies), and 0s (any coin not present) and focus on both multiplication and division. An active way to explore some of these facts is to sing "Head, Shoulders, Knees, and Toes" with students and then to ask them to figure out how many of each body part there are for different numbers of students. They can even complete a table like the one shown in Figure 4.11 to examine the patterns in the ensuing class discussion.

Notice that the columns do not include all the options. This is intentional, so that you can observe whether students are skip counting, are using a strategy, or "just know" the facts. If you want to include 5s, follow up with asking how many toes on just the right foot, which also is a great way to help students see the relationship between the 10s facts and 5s facts!

Finally, a great game for targeting foundational facts is Pathways. In this game, you choose the facts you want students to practice and place those products on the game board (this can also be played with addition facts, recording sums on the game board). Because students are seeking products on the game board, they are also exploring division facts related to the foundational multiplication facts.

FIGURE 4.11	Multiplication Patterns in "Head, Shoulders, Knees, and Toes"							
	Number of People							
	0	1	2	4	5	8	9	10
Body Part								
Head	0	1	2	4	5			
Shoulders	0	2	4	8	10	16		
Knees	0	2						
Toes	0	10						

GAME 31

MULTIPLICATION PATHWAYS ● ● ● ●

For two players, you need: two paper clips or clear counters, pencil (or marker, if the game board is laminated), 4 × 6 game board with foundational fact products in the squares:

	0	40	20	3	2	5	
S	8	10	5	30	0	10	F
T							I
A	5	20	8	50	6	20	N
R							I
T	10	4	0	10	30	12	S
	0	1	2	3	4	5	6	10	H

How to play: Players work as a team to find a pathway across the game board from left to right. To begin, players place paper clips on two different numbers at the bottom of the board, trying to make a product shown in the first column on the left. They then shade in that box on the game board. Next, they must decide which of the two clips to move to form the product directly to the right of the shaded square, either horizontally or diagonally. They cannot move vertically or backwards! The object is to get all the way across the game board. If they cannot form a product on any given move, they must go back to Start and try again.

Possible variations: Factors at the bottom of the board and products in the squares can be changed. To practice multiplication square products, allow students to place both clips on the same number.

Summary

When students first begin solving multiplication problems, they often use skip counting or repeated addition to find the products. Let's revisit the problem from the beginning of this chapter.

> Anna is making bags for her birthday party guests. She has 6 bags and wants to put 5 treats in each bag. How many treats will Anna need in all?

At first, students will likely solve this problem by skip counting by 5s (5, 10, 15, 20, 25, 30) or by repeated addition (5 + 5 + 5 + 5 + 5 + 5). Although these are appropriate approaches in the early stages, they are Phase 1 approaches because they are essentially based in counting. Unfortunately, many students never progress beyond using skip counting as their main approach to solving multiplication facts and thus never really develop true fluency with multiplication.

In summary, helping students progress from Phase 1 to Phase 3 with the foundational facts requires several key elements to be in place:

- Connecting the facts to students' understanding of addition and place value
- Using quick looks to connect equal groups or arrays to facts (and vice versa)
- Encouraging the use of mental images to "picture" facts such as 0×5 and 1×5
- Helping students to see relationships among facts, including commutativity and the relationship between 5s and 10s
- Providing significant practice through activities and games where students are connecting groups or arrays to the corresponding multiplication equations

This chapter has placed the foundational multiplication facts in this order: 2s, 10s, 5s, 1s, 0s, and squares; however, these need to be thought of in a cumulative manner. When focusing on 0s and 1s, you may play How Low Can You Go?, but you may also have stations where students are playing games with 2s, 5s, or 10s. As students are solving story problems, exploring quick looks, and playing games, you are listening and watching to see if they are counting (Phase 1) or becoming automatic (Phase 3). Tools to help you monitor and track students' mastery of the foundational facts for multiplication is the focus of Chapter 6. Once students have reached Phase 3 (automaticity) with the foundational multiplication facts, they are ready to start developing mathematically rich derived fact strategies—the focus of Chapter 5.

5

Derived Fact Strategies for Multiplication and Division

In comparison to addition, derived fact strategies for multiplication are more complex, as they involve decomposing *groups*, not just a single number. Ironically, however, explicit instruction of derived fact strategies for multiplication are less emphasized in standards and in textbooks than strategies for addition facts. The unfortunate consequence is that many students (and even adults) never become automatic with all multiplication facts (or learn efficient strategies for multidigit multiplication problems). A lack of automaticity with multiplication facts makes computing with fractions, simplifying algebraic expressions, and many other higher-level mathematical skills significantly more difficult for students.

Once again, we connect the five fundamentals of basic fact fluency to the material in this chapter.

1. **Mastery must focus on fluency.** If students don't know a fact like 6 × 7, they need options for finding the product efficiently. The ability to choose and use strategies flexibly are must-haves for fluency and mastery.
2. **Fluency develops in three phases.** This chapter focuses on moving students from skip counting (Phase 1) to strategies (Phase 2) to mastery (Phase 3) with the derived multiplication facts. Phase 2 is the major focus of this chapter.

3. **Foundational facts must precede derived facts.** Assuming that the foundational facts have become automatic, this chapter focuses on decomposing with those facts to derive the remaining multiplication facts.

4. **Timed tests do not assess fluency.** Assessments must be chosen that will allow teachers to monitor which strategies are used by each student and how efficiently they are used; timed tests do not show either.

5. **Students need substantial and enjoyable practice.** The final section of this chapter offers a collection of strategy games, providing opportunities for students to practice different ways of decomposing factors, eventually developing automaticity with these strategies and with all the basic facts.

Multiplication Derived Fact Strategies

Multiplication fact strategies help reinforce the meaning of multiplication as equal groups. If students are demonstrating automaticity with most of the foundational facts, then it is time to help them develop strategies (Phase 2) to facilitate learning the remaining multiplication facts. As illustrated in the Multiplication Fact Flexible Learning Progression (see Figure 5.1), foundational facts (especially 1s, 2s, and 5s) are very useful in generating the remaining facts.

As you explore these ideas in this chapter, please note two key principles of multiplication derived fact strategies:

- The *equal groups* meaning of multiplication must remain at the forefront of strategy work.
- Manipulating representations showing equal groups or arrays can be helpful for keeping track of steps.

Because the two factors in a multiplication fact can have different meanings (the number of groups or the amount in each group), it is advisable to alter only one factor when beginning to use multiplication fact strategies. For most students, it is easiest to alter the number of groups and then compensate by adding or subtracting some groups.

Doubling

Addition doubles are easier facts for many students to learn (see Chapter 2). The idea of doubling is revisited when teaching the 2s multiplication facts, the first set of multiplication foundational facts (see Chapter 4). However, Doubling as a multiplication derived fact strategy applies to facts other than 2s. The reasoning process involves first *halving* one factor, multiplying this value by the other factor, and then *doubling* the partial product. Doubling works for all 4s facts, making them a good place to begin. Figure 5.2 contains a 3rd grader's illustration of this process with 4 × 8.

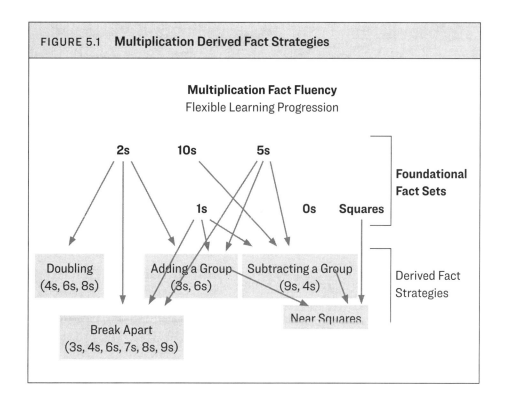

FIGURE 5.1   **Multiplication Derived Fact Strategies**

The student halved the 4 and then multiplied each half by 8. The resulting partial products were added together to yield the final result: 4 × 8 = (2 × 8) + (2 × 8).

Students can be encouraged to develop the Doubling strategy through carefully chosen quick looks. Because time is so limited during a quick look, students are motivated to discover efficient ways of decomposing the image, and halving and doubling quickly becomes one way of making sense of these images. Consider the pair of images in Figure 5.3. A teacher might begin by showing the image on the left, using the quick looks routine, and then follow with the image on the right. Some students will recognize the doubled image and will describe doubling the original total to find the new total; that is, the first image showed a total of 12 dots, and the new image is double that, so there are 12 + 12, or 24 total dots.

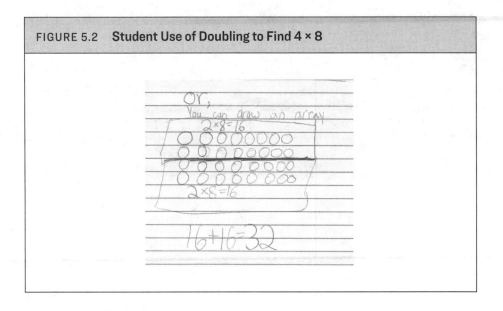

FIGURE 5.2   **Student Use of Doubling to Find 4 × 8**

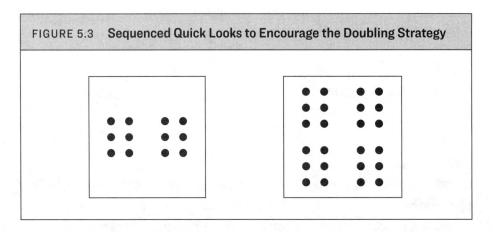

FIGURE 5.3   **Sequenced Quick Looks to Encourage the Doubling Strategy**

Once the Doubling strategy emerges, it can then be highlighted and recorded in words and number sentences, and students can be encouraged to apply it to future images.

Eventually, students come to reason more abstractly using doubling. Figure 5.4 shows what the mental process looks like.

FIGURE 5.4 Doubling Strategy Reasoning	
Mental Process in Symbols	**What Students Might Think or Say as They Solve**
$4 \times 6 = ?$	I know that 4 times a number is the same as multiplying the number by 2 twice.
$2 \times (2 \times 6) = ?$	I double 6 (multiply it by 2). I know that equals 12.
$2 \times 12 = 24$	I now double 12. I know that equals 24.

Note that the process requires recognizing that multiplying by 4 is the same as multiplying by 2 twice, as well as intuitively applying the associative property: $(2 \times 2) \times 6 = 2 \times (2 \times 6)$. Fours are the most straightforward in applying the Doubling strategy (double and double again), but Doubling can be used for many facts. Any fact containing at least one even factor can be broken into halves and then doubled. A student's thinking for 7×6, for example, is outlined in Figure 5.5.

FIGURE 5.5 Using the Doubling Strategy for 7×6	
Mental Process in Symbols	**What Students Might Think or Say as They Solve**
$7 \times 6 = ?$	I don't know 7×6, but 6 is even, so I can find 7×3 and then double it.
$7 \times 3 \times 2 = ?$	I know 7×3 is 21.
$21 \times 2 = 42$	I double 21, and it equals 42.

If both factors are even (e.g., 8×6), the student can pick either one to decompose.

The game Fixed Factor War can be adapted to work on any group of multiplication facts. However, using an **even** fixed factor, such as 4 or 8, can encourage the Doubling strategy in particular.

GAME 32
FIXED FACTOR WAR

● ● ● ●

For each pair of players, you need: deck of playing cards with king and jacks removed (ace = 1, queen = 0)

How to play: Identify a factor and place a card with that number faceup in the middle. Players divide the rest of the cards equally, shuffle them, and place them facedown. At the same time, both players turn up the top card and determine the product of their card and the factor in the middle. Each partner takes turns saying the full multiplication sentence, and both decide if the products are correct. You may wish to encourage students to explain how they used halving and doubling to find the product. The player who correctly states the greater product gets both players' cards. (The middle card stays.) If there is a tie, a "war" is declared, and partners repeat the process, with the winner taking all played cards. The player with the most cards wins.

Possible variations: Play Fixed Addend War. Play for a set time. Use numeral cards instead of playing cards. Have students record their equations. (This helps with accountability.)

Adding a Group

With addition, it is fairly intuitive for many students to start with a nearby known fact and simply add on one more, as in finding 5 + 6 by adding one more to 5 + 5. Multiplication, however, is not nearly as intuitive, as it involves manipulating *groups* instead of single numbers. Yet the idea of adding a group to a known fact is a very useful strategy, and time spent developing it is time well invested. Initially, the Adding a Group strategy can be helpful for deriving the 3s facts (adding one group to the related 2s fact) and the 6s facts (adding one group to the related 5s fact). However, that is just the beginning, as students can apply this strategy to any fact when they know a nearby fact. The reasoning shown in Figure 5.6 illustrates how solving 6s facts can begin with the related 5s facts.

Notice that this approach requires strategic planning. First, students must consider which factor they might decompose. Then, they need to know the size of the group they have broken off. In the example in Figure 5.6, students might mistakenly think they need to add 1 back on (instead of one group).

FIGURE 5.6 Adding a Group Strategy Reasoning	
Mental Process in Symbols	**What Students Might Think or Say as They Solve**
6 × 7 = __	I don't know 6 × 7, but I do know my 5s, so I can first find 5 × 7.
5 × 7 + 7 = ?	I know 5 groups of 7 is 35.
35 + 7 = 42	I have to add one more group of 7 to 35 and that equals 42.

One way of helping students make sense of the Adding a Group strategy is to use *sequenced number stories*. A sequenced number story is a story that comes in two parts, with the first part involving known facts and the second part providing a change in the story so that another group is added (Kling & Bay-Williams, 2015). Students are prompted to build from their solution to the first part to determine the final solution. Consider this example:

1. Becky has 2 bags of library books. Each bag contains 7 library books. How many books does Becky have in all?
2. Becky finds one more bag of library books in her closet, which also contains 7 library books. How many books does Becky have now? Use what you already know to figure it out.

Rather than starting over and drawing 3 groups of 7, students can simply start from the known fact of 2 × 7 = 14 and add one more group to get 14 + 7 = 21. Students can also use models or drawings to help keep track of the two steps of the story, as shown in Figure 5.7.

Once students have had practice with sequenced number stories, they need opportunities to apply this strategy so that, when faced with an unknown fact, they can identify a related and known helper fact to start from. This often requires some facilitation from the teacher, as shown in the following discussion about 6 × 8.

A class of 3rd graders has just finished playing a multiplication facts card game. Mrs. K. asks Harrison if there were any facts his group had trouble with.

Harrison: I had a tough time with 6 times 8.

Mrs. K.: Hmmm, that can be a tricky one. What did you try to do to figure it out?

Harrison: I wasn't sure. I tried counting by 8s, but that took a while.

Mrs. K.: Can you think of anything close by that you already know that might help you?

Harrison: I'm really good with my 5s and my 7s.

Mrs. K.: Okay, so can you think of a 5s fact or a 7s fact that you know that is close to 6 times 8?

Harrison: Well, I know that 5 times 8 equals 40—that's easy.

Mrs. K.: So if 5 times 8, or 5 groups of 8, equals 40, how could we use that to figure out what 6 groups of 8 would have?

Harrison: I guess I have to add… it would have to be more… I have to add 8 more. That would give me 48.

Mrs. K.: How did you know you needed to add 8?

Harrison: Because if I know that 5 groups of 8 made 40, I just need one more group, so I need 8 more. Forty plus 8 equals 48, so 48 is my answer.

FIGURE 5.7   Student Representation of Adding a Group

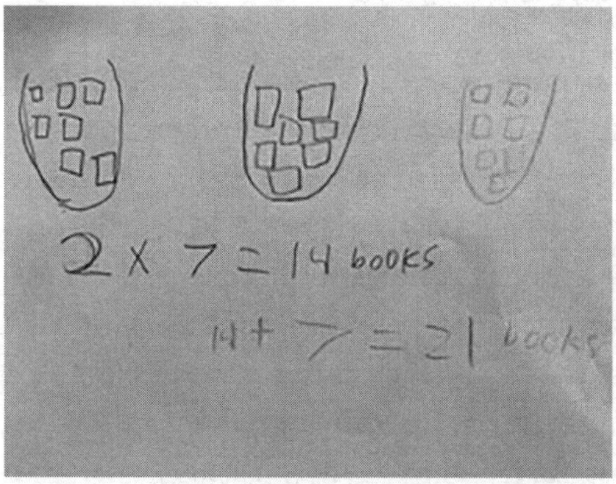

Mrs. K. makes sure that Harrison's explanation focuses on equal groups. Without a solid concept of multiplication as equal groups, students may think to start with the helper fact 5 × 8 = 40 but not know what to do next. Do they add another 5 or another 8, or do they need to add 6 because that number is no longer in the equation? With such struggles, pointing back to the *meaning* of the multiplication as 6 groups of 8 helps set students in the right direction. Quick sketches, such as the one in Figure 5.8, can also help students see how to break apart one group.

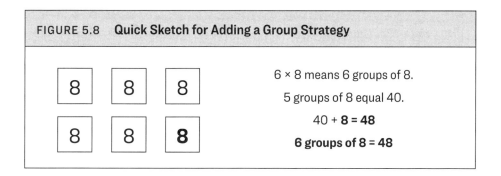

FIGURE 5.8   Quick Sketch for Adding a Group Strategy

6 × 8 means 6 groups of 8.

5 groups of 8 equal 40.

40 + **8** = **48**

6 groups of 8 = 48

Subtracting a Group

The counterpart to the Adding a Group strategy is, of course, Subtracting a Group. Students can explore this strategy in much the same way they discovered Adding a Group—through sequenced number stories. Figure 5.9 provides an example that uses an array.

Ask students to solve part 1, drawing an array to represent the problem. Then, pose part 2 and encourage students to alter the array they already created, rather than draw a new array.

Subtracting a Group is particularly useful for mastering the 9s, but it can also be applied to other situations. Students who are fluent with the 5s facts can subtract a group to determine the related 4s facts. Also, 8s facts can be solved by starting from the related 10s fact and subtracting *two* groups:

8 × 7 = ?

10 × 7 = 70

2 × 7 = 14

70 − 14 = 56, so 8 × 7 = 56

FIGURE 5.9   **Sequenced Number Story for Subtracting a Group**

1. Manuel is planting his garden. He has room for 10 rows of plants. He can put 4 plants in each row. How many plants can Manuel fit in his garden?

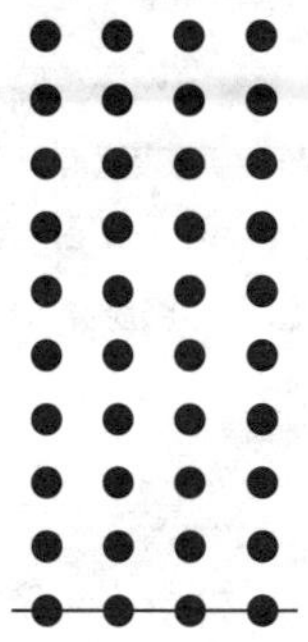

2. A row of plants was eaten by rabbits. Now Manuel only has 9 rows with 4 plants in each row. Use what you already know to figure out how many plants Manuel has in his garden now.

A word of caution regarding the 9s facts: we have encountered many students, teachers, and parents who share a finger trick as a means for learning the 9s facts. Although this trick works, it has several limitations:

- Students don't understand why the trick works.
- Students lose out on an opportunity to develop flexibility, efficiency, and appropriate strategy use (i.e., fluency) with the 9s facts.
- Students often make mistakes with their fingers and arrive at an incorrect answer.
- It can't be applied for 9s beyond single digit multiplication (e.g., 9 × 12). Notice that Subtracting a Group can be used—just start with 10 groups of 12.

Many games provide practice for all or most multiplication facts. Although these are valuable, after a new strategy is introduced, it can be particularly helpful to use games that target that strategy. The game Strive to Derive is particularly designed to encourage students in their use of the Adding a Group and Subtracting a Group strategies.

Near Squares

The Near Squares strategy is really a special case of the Adding a Group and Subtracting a Group strategies, since students are adding to or subtracting from a square number. We include it as a separate strategy, however, because students tend to master at least some multiplication squares easily and therefore benefit from explicit instruction on using those squares to generate some of the toughest facts. For example, a particularly challenging fact is 7 × 8 or 8 × 7, which can be solved by Adding a Group of 7 to 7 × 7 (49) or Subtracting a Group of 8 from 8 × 8 (64) to get 56. Organization is key to deciding how to compensate correctly, though. To help students remember whether they are Adding a Group of 7 or Subtracting a Group of 8, invite students to create (or visualize) a square array and add or subtract a row as needed, as illustrated in Figure 5.10.

GAME 33
STRIVE TO DERIVE   ● ● ● ●

For two to four players, you need: array cards (showing arrays for the 3s, 6s, 9s, and 10s that are labeled with the corresponding facts), one marker per student (uncooked spaghetti, coffee stirrer, thin straw or skewer, etc.)

How to play: Spread out the array cards so they can be seen. Players take turns selecting an array for the person on their right. That player must find a way to use his marker to partition the array into two or use one of the 10s array cards (placed under the selected card) to show the Subtracting a Group strategy. If the player is able to illustrate and explain how to use Adding a Group or Subtracting a Group to find the fact, that player earns a point. Return the array to the middle, and the next player has a turn. Play until someone scores 10 points.

> Example: A player is given a 9 × 6 array card. She pulls the 10 × 6 array card and places it underneath to show that 10 × 6 − 1 × 6 = 9 × 6. She could also place her marker to show 5 × 9 + 1 × 9 = 6 × 9.

Possible variations: Require that students divide the array so that one of the parts is a 5s fact (Strive to Derive by 5). For example, 6 × 7 could be shown as 5 × 7 + 1 × 7 or 6 × 5 + 6 × 2. Roll two 10-sided dice to determine the dimensions of the array. Players either find that array in the cards or draw it before partitioning it. (This can be played as a team or in competition.)

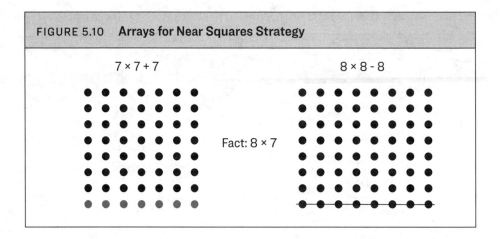

FIGURE 5.10   Arrays for Near Squares Strategy

7 × 7 + 7

8 × 8 - 8

Fact: 8 × 7

Break Apart

This strategy truly is the bottom line, the capstone, the destination. The Break Apart strategy is not only a way to generate any unknown fact from known facts, but it is also significant because it uses the key mathematical concept of decomposition. In reality, all the other derived fact strategies are actually special cases of the Break Apart strategy. If this is so, then, why not just start here and forget the rest? Although Break Apart is highly versatile, it is also more challenging because students have to think about which factor to break apart and how to break it apart. When students experience using the Doubling and Adding/Subtracting a Group strategies, they have practice with decomposing one factor in a designated way. They are then ready to think about breaking apart a factor in any way they find useful. In other words, the other derived fact strategies serve as scaffolds to the broader idea of decomposition. Thinking about *which* factor to break apart and then *how* to break it apart takes time and much experience.

Because students are choosing how to break apart a factor, a rectangle can be a more convenient model than an array. Arrays can be tedious to draw as compared to rectangles, and students can approximate a length without worrying about how many objects or what size the rectangle is. Thus, students will be more efficient applying the Break Apart strategy once they have become familiar with the concept of area and how to determine areas of rectangles efficiently. This may require you to reconsider how you sequence topics in your curriculum. Placing a unit on area between instruction on the foundational multiplication facts and instruction on the derived fact strategies not only serves this purpose but also provides additional time to practice foundational facts.

The use of concrete representations and real-world contexts can greatly enhance students' ability to make sense of the Break Apart strategy. Consider how the garden problem below illustrates this idea.

> You are planting a garden in a 6' × 8' rectangle. You want to plant 2 types of vegetables. Find all the ways you can put a fence through the garden to make 2 smaller rectangles (one for each vegetable). Make sure your cuts create only whole-number lengths. Use graph paper to show all the possible gardens.

A group of students who worked on this problem (see Figure 5.11) used several precut, 6 × 8 rectangular grids, construction paper, scissors, and glue. Each solution was created by cutting apart a rectangular grid into two smaller rectangles. Students recorded the related number sentences in their pictures.

FIGURE 5.11   **Students Solving the Garden Problem**

The garden problem provides an engaging, concrete first encounter with the Break Apart strategy. Eventually, students can recognize that it is helpful to break apart a challenging multiplication fact into two smaller helper facts that they already know well. Often this may involve 2s, 5s, or 10s facts, but the actual known facts will vary depending on the individual student.

Games that involve arrays and rectangles can help students practice the Break Apart strategy, especially if you encourage them to use it instead of skip counting to find the products or areas.

GAME 34
CROSSED WIRES ● ● ● ●

For two players, you need: deck of playing cards with queens (0), aces (1), 2s, 3s, 4s, and 5s, paper and pencil for each student

How to play: Shuffle the cards and place them facedown. Each player takes one card from the deck. This card tells how many horizontal lines ("wires") to draw on their paper. (The lines should be about 4 inches long.) Next, each player draws a second card and draws that number of vertical lines, crossing these "wires" over the first set. For example, drawing a 3 card and then a 4 card would look like this:

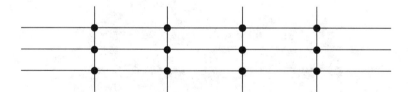

Each player determines how many crossed wires they have (points of intersection). If they don't know the fact, they must find some way to partition the array to find the product. For example, in this array, a student might double 4 (8) and add one more 4 to equal 12. Players record their products at the bottom of their paper. Play for five rounds. The winner is the person who has the most crossed wires in all.

Possible variation: Set one of the factors to practice a single fact set. Players draw that number of lines and then draw a card to determine how many crossed wires to draw. Players must then use the Break Apart strategy to determine the number of intersections.

GAME 35

RECTANGLE FIT   ● ● ● ●

For the class, you need: two dice, one game board per player (grid paper that is approximately 10 units × 20 units), one pencil per student

How to play: The teacher (or selected leader) rolls two dice. Each student chooses a place on the game board to shade a rectangle with the dimensions rolled. For example, if the leader rolls 4 and 6, each student decides the location and the orientation where they can best fit a 4 × 6 rectangle on the grid paper. Students record the related multiplication fact inside the rectangle. The leader continues to roll, and students mark out the rectangle somewhere on their grids. Rectangles cannot overlap. When students can no longer fit a rectangle with the given dimensions, they are out of the game. The last students in the game are the winners.

Possible variations: Use 10-sided dice with a game board with more unit squares (centimeter grid). Students who are out of the game can record the fact for which they lost on the back of the page but then may keep playing (unofficially).

A major reason for developing the Break Apart strategy is that it extends beyond basic facts to support fluency with other multiplication situations. For example, 15 × 8 can be decomposed into 10 × 8 (80) and 5 × 8 (40), which add to 120; alternately, the factor of 8 can be halved to yield 15 × 4 (60), which is then doubled to find the total of 120.

With either the basic facts or with greater factors, the Break Apart strategy uses the distributive property of multiplication over addition: $a \times (b + c) = a \times b + a \times c$. Even without having formal knowledge of this property, students can develop a deep, intuitive understanding of it as they model and apply the Break Apart strategy.

Related Division Facts

Knowing multiplication facts does not automatically lead to knowing division facts, just as knowing addition doesn't guarantee knowing subtraction facts. Division facts are the hardest of the four operations for students, and there are several reasons for their struggles. First, there is much less time built into curricula for learning related division facts. Insufficient practice results in students who do not know strategies for solving division problems. Second, unlike subtraction, there are not many strategies for solving division facts. In fact, research suggests there is only one: Think Multiplication (Kouba 1989; Mulligan & Mitchelmore, 1997; National Research Council, 2001; Thornton, 1978). Finally, and most importantly, when students use division beyond basic facts, they are often asked to think of a close-by fact, not an exact fact. Consider the example of 45 ÷ 6. Since 6 does not divide into 45 evenly, it requires the student to think, "Six times what number gives me an answer close to 45?" In this case, a student must know the 6s multiplication facts and recognize that 6 × 7 = 42 is the closest fact that has a product less than 45.

Think Multiplication

Division facts are best learned by using the Think Multiplication strategy. For example, to solve 49 ÷ 7 = ?, we ask, "What times seven equals 49?" Missing-factor story problems can help students interpret division in terms of multiplication. The missing factor can be the number of groups or the size of the group, as illustrated by these examples.

- The 3rd grade class is preparing coloring kits for the preschool. Each bag needs to have 5 crayons. How many bags can be filled if there are 45 crayons?
- Two children are sharing 18 crayons. How many will each child get?

The first story can be represented as __ × 5 = 45 (number of groups unknown), or as 45 ÷ 5 = __. The second story can be represented as 2 × __ = 18 (size of group unknown), or 18 ÷ 2 = __. Games can provide an engaging context for students to practice finding factors for a given product.

GAME 36

THE FACTOR GAME   ● ● ● ●

For two players, you need: one Factor Game board (5 × 6 grid, numbered 1 to 30), pencil or counters to mark out or cover spaces

1	2	3	4	5
6	7	8	9	10
11	12	13	14	15
16	17	18	19	20
21	22	23	24	25
26	27	28	29	30

How to play: The first player chooses a number on the game board and marks or covers it. This is his score for the first round. The second player covers all the factors of the first player's number that are not yet covered and adds their values. This is her score for the first round. (Example: The first player selects 15, which is his score. The second player covers 1, 3, and 5, which are the remaining factors of 15. This gives her a score of 9.) The next round begins when the second player chooses a number, and the first player covers any not covered factors left on the board. Play continues in this manner. If at any time a player selects a number that has no uncovered factors, the opponent does not get any points. The game ends when all the numbers are covered. Points are added, and the player with the greater sum wins.

Possible variations: Use a 7 × 7 game board with values 1 through 49. For older students, use a 10 × 10 game board with values 1 through 100.

Close-By Division Facts

Students are expected to know close-by division facts (compatible numbers) for most long division algorithms and for estimation with division, yet few resources provide opportunities for students to think about them. That is where games come in. Because they can be played over and over again, games such as The Right Price provide much needed experience with this strategy.

GAME 37
THE RIGHT PRICE   ● ● ● ●

For two to four players, you need: two dice, deck of playing cards with face cards removed (ace = 1)

How to play: Deal six cards to each player and place the rest facedown in a draw pile. The first player rolls the dice and uses the two numbers to decide a price. (For example, a 2 and a 5 can be $25 or $52.) The other players use the cards in their hand to form a multiplication fact that comes as close to the price as possible *without going over*. The player with the closest product scores 12 points. If there is a tie, the players divide the points evenly. Used cards are discarded, and new cards are drawn. Continue play until the deck is gone. The player with the highest score wins.

Possible variations: Use two 10-sided dice to determine prices. Use cards from the deck to determine prices.

Using Games to Achieve Mastery

It is not enough to introduce and discuss multiplication and division fact strategies, even in the intuitive ways described in this chapter. Purposeful, frequent practice is needed for students to develop the fluency needed to progress to Phase 3 with all multiplication facts. This practice can be targeted toward specific facts or strategies, such as in the games Fixed Factor War and Strive to Derive, or it can involve more general practice of all multiplication facts.

One way to use facts games purposefully is to incorporate strategy discussion either before or after game play. For example, before playing Multiplication Salute or The Product Game, the teacher can ask students to imagine a player is stuck on a particular fact and have them suggest good strategies that person could use to figure out the product quickly. Alternately, a teacher might close game play by bringing the class back together and having them brainstorm strategies for solving a fact that several groups had difficulty with during the game. Within a few minutes, the class can brainstorm many reasonable strategies. This quick, fruitful discussion gets everyone in the mindset of seeking and applying strategies during the ensuing game play. The key is to make practice through games as meaningful and strategy-focused as possible.

GAME 38

MULTIPLICATION SALUTE

For three players, you need: deck of playing cards with kings and jacks removed (ace = 1, queen = 0)

How to play: Determine which of the three students will be the leader for the first draw. This player takes the deck (facedown) and hands each of the other two players a card. Without looking at the card, the two players place the cards on their foreheads facing outward, so the others can see it. The leader states the product of the two cards. The other two players must each determine the value of the cards on their foreheads, based on hearing the product and seeing one factor. Both players share how they determined their number. Rotate so that one of the other players is now the leader. Continue until the deck is gone.

Possible variations: Use only designated cards, such as 1–5 and 10 to start, or jacks and queens as 11s and 12s to extend. Score points by having the faster player keep the cards.

GAME 39

THE PRODUCT GAME

For two players, you need: two colors of chips or markers (if board is laminated), two paper clips, game board as shown

1	2	3	4	5	6
7	8	9	10	12	14
15	16	18	20	21	24
25	27	28	30	32	35
36	40	42	45	48	49
54	56	63	64	72	81

Factors: 1   2   3   4   5   6   7   8   9

How to play: The goal is to get four squares in a row (horizontally, vertically, or diagonally). To begin, the first player places both paper clips on any two factors below the table and covers or marks the corresponding product. The second player moves one paper clip and claims the square with the new product. Play continues as the two players try to get four in a row or block each other from getting four in a row.

Possible variations: Pair students in teams. Change the goal from getting four in a row to making a 2 × 2 square.

Games for All Four Operations

The need for basic fact fluency certainly doesn't end when students move to the next grade. Basic facts are utilized for so much higher-level mathematics that continued practice is essential. Furthermore, it is important to integrate practice across the four operations. There are three important reasons for this:

- It is common for students to confuse what it means to add 0 or 1 and what it means to multiply by 0 or 1. Mixed practice helps alleviate this confusion.
- Students compare the relative impact of the operations with whole numbers, seeing that multiplying by a number results in a greater increase than adding that number.
- Mixing the operations and recording the related equations provides experience with the order of operations and appropriate use of parentheses.

Here are a few fun strategy games that involve all four operations.

GAME 40
NET ZERO   ● ● ● ●

For groups of two to three players, you need: deck of playing cards with face cards removed (ace = 1), paper and pencil

How to play: The goal of the game is to generate equations equal to zero. Each player turns over five cards. Players then use these cards to create equations that equal zero and write the equations on their papers. They may use any number of cards and any of the four operations. The person with the most cards wins.

Possible variations: Pair students to work together as a team, attempting to generate 5 unique equations (or 10). Change the target from zero to another number. Give bonus points for equations that use division.

GAME 41

SOFTBALL HITS   ● ● ● ●

For two to three players, you need: three dice, game board with a drawing of a softball field (one per player)

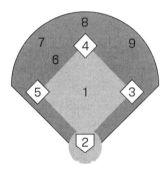

How to play: The goal of the game is to "hit" to every position, beginning with the pitcher (position 1) and going around the field in order. Players take turns rolling the three dice. They must use any two or all three of the numbers and any combination of operations to create an equation equal to 1. If the player can successfully create an equation equal to 1, he can try to use the same numbers to create an equation equal to 2, and so on. When he cannot create an equation for the desired number, he passes the dice to the next player. On his next turn, he begins where he left off. The first player to "hit" to every position wins the game.

Possible variations: Require that all three dice be used. Instead of giving a game board to each player, have them collaborate to gets hits to all positions. Use 10-sided dice. Allow students to mark positions off in any order.

GAME 42

THREE DICE TAKE ● ● ● ●

For two players, you need: three dice, counters in two different colors (20 of each) or two colors of markers (if game board is laminated), game board numbered 0–39, as shown

0	1	2	3	4	5	6	7
8	9	10	11	12	13	14	15
16	17	18	19	20	21	22	23
24	25	26	27	28	29	30	31
32	33	34	35	36	37	38	39

How to play: This is a strategy game where players try to get spaces that are worth the most points. Players score 1 point for taking an unoccupied space and additional points for any surrounding spaces that were already taken. For example, in the illustration below, the point value for the highlighted space is 6: 1 point for the space itself (19) and 5 more points (1 point for each) for the taken spaces.

~~10~~	~~11~~	~~12~~
~~18~~	(19)	20
26	27	~~28~~

Players take turns rolling the dice and using all three numbers with any combination of operations to get a number on the game board. Play until the board is full or until time is up. The person with the higher score wins the game.

Possible variations: Mark six to eight spaces before players make their first move (to jump start the strategic selection of spaces). Pair students into teams and play with two teams per game board.

Summary

The path to multiplication and division fact fluency can be a bumpy one for many students. It requires a deep mathematical understanding of how to decompose factors and retain an equivalent expression. Fluency with all multiplication facts requires automaticity not only with foundational multiplication facts but also with addition and subtraction facts. This requires a great deal of time, effort, and patience, both on the part of students and teachers. In addition, these efforts must continue throughout the school year and not be relegated to a particular unit.

This investment over time, however, has great payoffs. The traditional approach of learning multiplication facts, which relies heavily on rote memorization, may result in students forgetting or confusing facts. An investment in strategy instruction means that students can regenerate a fact they have forgotten without resorting to skip counting. Additionally and significantly, hurrying through the facts without teaching decomposition makes it harder to understand the place value strategies and algorithms for multidigit multiplication and division. Do you need to find 39 × 15? Start with 40 × 15, which can be mentally computed (600), and subtract a group of 15 to get 585. An algorithm isn't needed to find 16 × 25 because it is the double of 8 × 25, or 200. In fact, because these strategies are based on fundamental mathematical properties, they even extend to rational numbers; for example, $8 \times 2\frac{1}{4}$ can be solved efficiently by decomposing it into 8 × 2 = 16 and $8 \times \frac{1}{4} = 2$ to find the total (18). Notice that each of these examples are *more efficient* than traditional algorithms. Focusing on strategies during the mastering of basic facts not only leads to fluency with basic facts but also prepares students to be fluent with multiplication and division in all applications. Finally, and perhaps most important, when value is placed on developing sound mathematical strategies, not on rote memorization, students understand that mathematics involves reasoning and strategizing about numbers. Fluency is not just a measure of mathematical skill; it is a mindset.

The first chapter of this book introduced the notion of fluency as comprising four components: flexibility, accuracy, efficiency, and appropriate strategy use. We truly believe that the focus on strategies, accompanied by examples, quick looks, and games, embody this rich definition of what it means to "do math." In the next two chapters, as we turn our attention to assessment, we once again delve into the importance of all four components of fluency, beginning with assessing foundational fact sets (Chapter 6) and then derived fact strategies (Chapter 7).

6

Assessing Foundational Facts

Foundational facts must be known before students can develop derived fact strategies (Fundamental #3). The foundational fact sets in the flexible learning progressions are necessary for later development of derived fact strategies.

Addition

- +/− 0, 1, 2
- Doubles
- Combinations of 10
- 10 + __

Multiplication

- 2s, 10s, and 5s
- 1s and 0s
- Squares

The focus of this chapter is determining which foundational fact sets a student knows and then considering what might be next steps to support that student on the journey to automaticity with all facts. Given the potential limitations and harms of timed testing, many teachers have asked, "What else can I do? I have to assess my kids." We live in a data-driven world, and the collection of data begins early; however, this doesn't mean timed testing is necessary. Instead, assessments such as observations, interviews, journal writing, strategy quizzes, and self-assessment provide more accurate and specific data for all four components of fluency (Bay-Williams & Kling, 2015). The key is to utilize the tools described in this chapter to make such assessment informative and manageable.

This chapter connects to the five fundamentals in these ways:

1. **Mastery must focus on fluency.** Selecting appropriate strategies and having flexibility with all basic facts is completely dependent upon automaticity and facility with the foundational fact sets.

2. **Fluency develops in three phases.** This chapter provides formative assessment tools to monitor students' progress from Phase 1 to Phase 3 for the foundational facts.

3. **Foundational facts must precede derived facts.** That is the reason for this chapter. The tools in this chapter can help you determine which foundational facts a student still needs to know before moving on to derived facts.

4. **Timed tests do not assess fluency.** This chapter offers alternative assessments that can be used instead of timed testing.

5. **Students need substantial and enjoyable practice.** Numerous ideas are shared in this chapter for monitoring students' progress while they engage in meaningful activities.

Observations

Providing time for game play is critical; students need practice, and games provide an engaging alternative to the drudgery of worksheets and flash cards. Games are not only valuable for practice; they also provide an excellent opportunity for formative assessment. The first two strategies discussed in this chapter, observations and interviews, can work seamlessly into a game-based approach to practice. As students play games and discuss their strategies, it is possible to listen and record data on what each student knows.

During game play, circulate with an observation tool on your tablet or clipboard. It is not necessary to assess *every student every time* a game is played. That is unrealistic. Instead, target a small group of students for assessment and collect data in an efficient manner by using observation charts. Each time the class plays a similar facts game, a different group of students can be observed, and before long a complete set of observation data will be collected.

The first step is to select an observation tool that fits what you are trying to assess. Three considerations are

- Which set(s) of facts or strategies are you assessing?
- Which components of fluency are you addressing?
- Are you assessing automaticity/mastery?

As you make decisions related to these considerations, many possible observation tools emerge. We can't share all the possibilities here, but we provide numerous examples that could certainly be adapted to other sets of facts or other goals as needed.

Which Foundational Facts Are Known?

Let's begin with observation tools that focus on the sets of foundational facts, like the two shown in Tool 1.

TOOL 1

Observation Tools for Foundational Fact Sets   ■   ■   ■   ■

Names	Foundational Fact Sets: Addition			
	+/– 0, 1, 2	Doubles	Combinations of 10	10 + __

Names	Foundational Fact Sets: Multiplication					
	2s	10s	5s	1s	0s	Squares

Within the cells, there is room to use codes such as an S for *sometimes;* a check mark for *usually;* or an asterisk for *really has it.* Alternately, brief notes can be recorded, such as *only smaller #s.*

Comprehensive foundational facts observation tools are particularly valuable first steps in assessing known and unknown facts. Determining which foundational facts need more attention is helpful in making instructional decisions and basic fact game selections. Of course, different students will have different known and unknown facts. The data gathered from the observations can be used to differentiate instruction by selecting games or other activities that specifically target the foundational facts each student most needs to learn, based on the learning progressions.

Assessing Accuracy and Automaticity

Students must reach automaticity with foundational fact sets before moving to derived fact strategies. Although students can be working on any of the foundational fact sets, the flexible learning progressions are sequenced in a way that prioritizes sets of facts that make sense to learn first. You should focus on these fact sets while establishing the parameters for observation.

The observation chart in Tool 2 can aid with recording whether a student gives automatic, accurate responses for the foundational addition and subtraction fact sets. For coding, use a ✓ for accuracy (correct) responses and an * for automaticity.

TOOL 2

Observation Tool for +/– 0, 1, 2

Names	Addition			Commutativity	Subtraction		
	+0	+1	+2		–0	–1	–2

If you want to assess automaticity, you simply need to count three seconds silently while you listen—*the student never needs to know that you are timing the response.* If the student answers correctly within three seconds, mark an asterisk on the chart to indicate the student demonstrated automaticity for that fact set.

Notice that there is a commutativity column for these facts. Some students will demonstrate automaticity for a fact when a number is the second addend (e.g., 3 + 1) but not when it is the first addend (e.g., 1 + 3). If students have not reached automaticity with facts presented in both ways, developing understanding of the commutative property must be a priority. Stories and jumps on the number line can help solidify this idea. Also, ask students to record equations as they play games and explicitly discuss the reversibility of the addends.

In the same way that automaticity with addition begins with the +/- 0, 1, 2 facts, automaticity with multiplication first focuses on 2s, 10s, and 5s. A critical issue with these facts is that students can skip count to find these products, sometimes within three seconds, but skip counting is not considered automatic. This is why the observation chart in Tool 3 has columns to note skip counting. Note the goal for automaticity is that the student does *not* skip count (N), but does recognize commutativity (Y) and is automatic (Y).

TOOL 3

**Observation Tool for ×
2s, 10s, and 5s**   ■   ■   ■   ■

Names	× 2			× 10			× 5		
	Skip Counts	Commutativity	Automaticity (within 3 seconds)	Skip Counts	Commutativity	Automaticity (within 3 seconds)	Skip Counts	Commutativity	Automaticity (within 3 seconds)

Commutativity is also important for multiplication. To observe whether students can recognize that two multiplication facts are equivalent requires games, activities, or interviews in which the facts appear both ways.

Focus on Individual Facts Within Foundational Fact Sets

Observation tools can be even more specific, focusing on just one fact set. This makes sense for the facts that are critical for later use with derived fact strategies, such as the combinations of 10 or doubles for addition. Charts like the one in Tool 4 can list the exact combinations the student must know, which the observer can mark to record accuracy and automaticity.

TOOL 4

Observation Tools for Combinations of 10 and Doubles ■ ■ ■ ■

Names	Combinations of 10 (Assuming Commutativity)			Key: ✓ = Accurate * = Automatic		
	0 and 10	1 and 9	2 and 8	3 and 7	4 and 6	5 and 5

Names	Doubles									Key: ✓ = Accurate * = Automatic
	0 + 0	1 + 1	2 + 2	3 + 3	4 + 4	5 + 5	6 + 6	7 + 7	8 + 8	9 + 9

Combinations of 10 must also be automatic when in the form of a missing addend, as in 7 + __ = 10. The combinations of 10 observation chart in Tool 4 can be renamed Missing Addends to Equal 10 to track student progress with these facts. Similarly, with doubles, students must be able to determine a missing double to make a given sum, as in __ + __ = 16. You might wish to relabel the Doubles Facts tool as Recognizing Doubles when assessing whether students can use this type of thinking to identify subtraction facts for doubles.

A look at the multiplication progression chart shows how necessary the 1s, 2s, and 5s facts are for derived fact strategies. Each of these warrants individual attention. A chart like the one shown in Tool 5 can list out the exact combinations the student must know, and the observer can mark the chart for accuracy and automaticity.

TOOL 5

Observation Tool for × 5s Facts   ■ ■ ■ ■

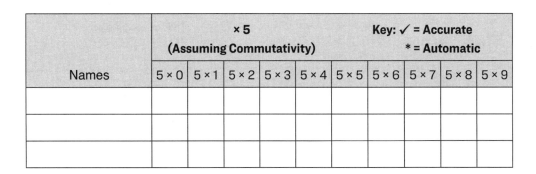

Names	×5 (Assuming Commutativity)									Key: ✓ = Accurate * = Automatic
	5 × 0	5 × 1	5 × 2	5 × 3	5 × 4	5 × 5	5 × 6	5 × 7	5 × 8	5 × 9

Regular use of observation charts throughout the school year provides highly specific and accurate measures of each student's progress toward mastery with foundational facts. Meanwhile, students are engaged in meaningful practice while you are assessing. The key to using observation as assessment is organization; the tools given in this chapter will help provide reasonable structure to facilitate this important practice.

Interviewing

Interviewing is arguably the most effective way to measure all four components of fluency, as well as automaticity. Although it requires some careful planning on the part of the teacher, there are various ways to go about scheduling interview assessments, with varying degrees of formality.

In-the-Moment Interviews

In-the-moment interviews occur as students are playing games or doing other activities. For example, a student may be engaged in a game and has just given a sum of 6. A question such as "How did you know the answer was 6?" can provide insights that you can capture as notes on an observation tool; also, prompting for an explanation communicates to students that you value their thinking. There are several possible questions that you can use to focus on strategy selection and flexibility:

- How did you figure it out?
- Is there another way you could figure it out?
- If someone didn't know the answer to ____, how would you tell them to figure it out?
- I see you used ____ strategy. When do you like to use that strategy?

These prompts can be taped to your clipboard as a reminder to ask students one of these questions as they solve story problems, use quick looks, or play games. The questions serve as formative assessments but also communicate to students the critical importance of these often-neglected aspects of fluency.

Sometimes students have trouble recalling what they *did*, but they are able to think aloud. In that case, rather than ask about a problem they finished, ask a student to think aloud while he solves a problem. (You will not want to use this technique, however, if you are assessing automaticity, as thinking aloud slows down their process and will give you an inaccurate measure of speed.)

One-on-One Interviews: Fact Sets

One-on-one interviews can also be done fairly quickly within the classroom. Inviting a student to a nearby desk and posing a few questions during game play, morning work, or downtimes during the school day works well for gathering data. Tool 6 contains a sample interview protocol that can be used for *any* of the foundational fact sets. The codes may be recorded on one of the observation tools shared earlier in this chapter or on one that you create.

TOOL 6

Two-Prompt Interview Protocol ■ ■ ■ ■

Two-Prompt Interview Protocol for Foundational Facts
PROMPTS:

1. What is __ + __ (or __ × __)? (Fill in with a foundational fact you wish to assess.)

2. How did you figure it out? (Ask this regardless of how quickly or accurately the student solves the fact.)

(Repeat with other facts related to the interview purpose.)

Mastery Code

* = Automatic (Add notation when student answers correctly within three seconds.)

Strategy Codes: Foundational Facts Sets

Addition	Multiplication
M = Must use models or objects to add **CA** = Counts all **CO** = Counts on **S** = Uses a strategy **R** = Recall (just knows the answer)	**SC** = Skip counts **S** = Uses a strategy **R** = Recall (just knows the answer)

As an example, consider conducting a quick interview to assess a student's progress toward automaticity for + 0, 1, and 2 facts. Possible flash cards (or facts to write on a whiteboard) might include the following:

- 4 + 1 =
- 2 + 2 =
- 5 + 2 =

- 7 + 0 =
- 11 + 1 =
- 16 + 1 =
- 1 + 3 =
- 0 + 3 =
- 1 + 6 =
- 1 + 8 =
- 0 + 5 =
- 12 + 2 =

Some flexibility may be needed as the interview progresses. For example, if the student is counting all (CA) for the first three facts, the interviewer has learned what was needed from the interview, and there is no need to ask the rest. However, the interviewer might ask, "Can you solve these in a way other than counting?" to be sure the student doesn't just need to be reminded of more efficient ways to find the sum. When conducting interviews with younger students, it is advisable to keep manipulatives such as counters out of sight unless a student demonstrates a need to use them. Otherwise, interviewees may reach for manipulatives even if they are not needed, thereby interfering with the purpose of the assessment.

Similarly, for multiplication, you may feel that students have their 2s and 10s to automaticity and just want to assess 5s, 0s, and 1s. A set for these facts might include the following:

- 8 × 1 =
- 0 × 6 =
- 5 × 5 =
- 7 × 1 =
- 8 × 5 =
- 5 × 6 =
- 1 × 3 =
- 0 × 3 =
- 2 × 5 =
- 3 × 5 =
- 0 × 5 =
- 5 × 7 =

If the student knows these facts from memory, an interview like this will take one minute or less. You can conclude by asking the student to tell you what she knows about facts multiplied by 0 or by 1 and how this compares to addition facts. If a student is struggling with these facts, perhaps confusing the multiplication properties related to 0s and 1s, then you can adapt the interview in the moment and ask the student to tell a story to match the fact or create an array to match the fact. In this way, you are not just gathering data about what students know but are also providing needed support to help strengthen the student's conceptual understanding of those facts.

Interview Records

Rather than using one of the observation tools shared earlier, you may wish to use an interview record to document each student's responses. Although this recording page has all the interview tasks, only one fact is recited (or shown) at a time. An addition record might focus on just one of the foundational fact sets or a combination of fact sets. An example focused on combinations of 10 is provided in Tool 7.

TOOL 7

Interview Record for Combinations of 10   ■   ■   ■   ■

Combinations of 10 Interview Record

Name: _____   Date: _____

(Ask students these facts verbally or show cards or whiteboard with each fact, one at a time.)

1. 5 + 5 = __   _____
2. 3 + 7 = __   _____
3. 10 + 4 = __   _____
4. 2 + 8 = __   _____
5. 3 + 6 = __   _____

(If using verbal prompts, ask the student to tell you how much to add to equal 10. Otherwise, show cards or whiteboard with each equation.)

6. 10 = 9 + __   _____
7. 8 + __ = 10   _____
8. 7 + __ = 10   _____
9. 10 = 6 + __   _____
10. 3 + __ = 10   _____

Strategy Codes
M = Models/objects used
CA = Counts all
CO = Counts on
S = Uses a strategy
R = Recall (just knows)

Mastery Code
* = Automatic

Notice that some "distractor" facts are included (numbers 3 and 5). This is because knowing combinations of 10 requires recognizing the combination in the first place. The answers for those two facts may be coded, but because the purpose of the interview is to determine whether the student recognizes and can accurately find combinations of 10, the accuracy of the distractor responses doesn't really matter. Finally, knowing combinations of 10 requires facility with knowing *how much is needed to make a combination of 10*. This skill is what students use for derived fact strategies, so analyzing the results must focus on whether the student is able to find the combination of 10 *and* find the missing addend to make 10. Alternately, you could express combinations of 10 facts as subtraction (changing 7 + __ = 10 to 10 − 7 = __) to assess subtraction more explicitly.

When using an interview record, if you notice that a student is consistently counting to find the missing numbers, you may decide to try the same fact coupled with a quick looks image. If you anticipate this may happen, have the corresponding ten frames ready for the interview and follow the quick looks routine. If a student *can* say the answer without counting for the quick look but cannot with the equations, then the student needs more opportunities to connect the images to the numbers. Ideas for facilitating this connection can be found in Chapter 2.

A multiplication record might also focus on just one of the foundational fact sets or a combination of fact sets. Tool 8 provides an example for the squares facts.

TOOL 8

Interview Record for
Multiplication Squares   ■   ■   ■   ■

Multiplication Squares Interview Record

Name: _____   Date: _____

(Ask students these facts verbally or show cards or whiteboard with each fact, one at a time.)

1. $2 \times 2 =$ __   _____
2. $5 \times 5 =$ __   _____
3. $1 \times 1 =$ __   _____
4. $4 \times 4 =$ __   _____
5. $0 \times 0 =$ __   _____
6. $6 \times 6 =$ __   _____

Strategy Codes
SC = Skip counts
S = Uses a strategy
R = Recall (just knows)

Mastery Code
* = Automatic

TOOL 8—*(continued)*

Interview Record for Multiplication Squares   ■ ■ ■ ■

7. 10 × 10 = __   _____
8. 3 × 3 = __   _____
9. 7 × 7 = __   _____
10. 8 × 8 = __   _____
11. 9 × 9 = __   _____

Notice that the first facts on the interview record are also 2s, 5s, and 1s; then it moves on to include squares that are not also in other foundational fact sets. Results of this interview may indicate that the student only knows the squares that are also in other foundational fact sets, only has automaticity with squares through 5 × 5, or is fluent with all multiplication squares. Each of these findings has different instructional next steps.

One-on-One Interviews: All Foundational Facts

Interviews can be used to determine whether a student has mastered the foundational facts in general. These interviews might include 10–15 questions across the different foundational fact sets and use a recording sheet, as shown in Tool 9. An interview to determine mastery of the foundational facts is a more accurate and less stressful assessment than a timed test.

These summative assessment interviews take longer and need to be structured differently so they go smoothly. One way to organize is to get assistance from a mathematics specialist or teaching assistant to conduct interviews in a side room or library space. Throughout the day (or week), students come and go, and the data are provided to the classroom teacher. Given that many state standards expect mastery of addition facts by the end of 2nd grade and multiplication facts by the end of 3rd grade, one idea is to schedule interviews midway through 2nd grade (addition) and 3rd grade (multiplication) to collect data on foundational facts, with plans to assess all types of facts (foundational and derived) at the end of the year.

TOOL 9
Mastery of Foundational Facts Records

■ ■ ■ ■

Foundational Addition Facts Interview Record

Name: _____   Date: _____

(Ask students these facts verbally or
show cards or whiteboard with each fact,
one at a time. Record codes in each box.)

6 + 6	8 + 2	4 + 4	7 + 7
9 - 1	2 + 6	0 + 7	5 - 2
3 + 3	4 + 6	9 + 9	4 - 0
3 + 7	1 + 9	5 + 5	10 - 2

Strategy Codes
M = Models/objects used
CA = Counts all
CO = Counts on
S = Uses a strategy
R = Recall (just knows)

Mastery Code
* = Automatic

Foundational Multiplication Facts Record

Name: _____   Date: _____

(Ask students these facts verbally or
show cards or whiteboard with each fact,
one at a time. Record codes in each box.)

10 × 6	8 × 2	2 × 4	5 × 3
9 × 1	2 × 6	0 × 7	1 × 8
3 × 10	4 × 5	3 × 3	4 × 0
5 × 7	1 × 6	5 × 5	7 × 7

Strategy Codes
SC = Skip counts
S = Uses a strategy
R = Recall (just knows)

Mastery Code
* = Automatic

Fluency Rubrics

You may wish to summarize the results from your interviews by assigning students an overall fluency score. This is far more meaningful than a score of correctness, as it involves scoring students on their progress toward being flexible (varying their choice of strategy) and efficient (using the best strategy for the numbers given, as well as working toward automaticity). Sample rubrics for fluency scores in addition and multiplication are shown in Tool 10.

TOOL 10

Rubrics for Foundational Fact Fluency

■ ■ ■ ■

General Fluency Rubric for Addition Foundational Facts

1	2	3	4
Uses counting strategies only	Fluent with facts within 5 or some foundational facts; counts for all others	Uses a blend of doubles, combinations of 10, and counting on; automatic with *some* foundational facts	Automatic with *most* or *all* of doubles, combinations of 10, and 10 + __ facts

General Fluency Rubric for Multiplication Foundational Facts

1	2	3	4
Uses skip counting strategies only	Fluent with some fact sets (e.g., 1s and 10s), skip counts for all others	Fluent with many of the facts across 2s, 10s, 5s, 1s, 0s, and squares; automatic with *some* foundational facts	Automatic with *most* or *all* of 2s, 5s, 10s, 1s, 0s, and possibly squares

Journal Writing

Beginning at a young age, students can be encouraged to express fact strategies using pictures, words, and number sentences. Whether working on addition facts or multiplication facts, doubles are an excellent topic for journaling because students can both illustrate and explain the idea of doubling, connecting it to the symbols for addition, multiplication, or both. This is illustrated in the sample prompts in Tool 11.

The benefits of journal writing are significant. Writing provides processing time and an opportunity for students to use pictures and words to demonstrate their thinking. Often, we begin with stories and ask students to find the answers, but journal writing lends itself to thinking in reverse. For example, you might pose the following prompts:

TOOL 11

Journal Writing
Prompts for Doubles

■   ■   ■   ■

Benefit/Purpose	Sample Prompts
Connecting to visuals or contexts	• Draw a picture or write a sentence about something that has two matching parts. Then write a doubles fact to match your picture or story.
Connecting to ten frames	• Write your favorite doubles fact. Draw it in the double ten frame. Why do you like this one? • Write a doubles fact you need to practice. Draw it in the double ten frame. How can you figure it out?
Commutativity (multiplication)	• Draw a picture that shows 2 × 6 and another picture that shows 6 × 2. Explain why these have the same product. • Luis says that 8 × 2 equals 2 × 8. Is he correct? How do you know?
Reflecting on the facts	• Write out the first six doubles facts. What pattern do you notice in the answers? How does that help you to figure out the next doubles fact? • Rachael says 7 + 7 = 15. Is she right? How do you know?
Connecting to subtraction/division	• Is 12 the answer to a doubles fact? Which fact(s)? • How do you know if a number is the sum/product for a doubles fact?

- Write a story that fits this problem: [insert foundational fact, such as 7 + 3 or 6 × 5].
- Write a story OR draw a picture that shows why 3 + 4 = 4 + 3 (or 5 × 4 = 4 × 5).
- Nicolas solved 5 × 6 by thinking of 10 × 3. Draw a picture to show why this works. Explain your thinking.

As these examples demonstrate, journal prompts provide much more information as to what students know about the facts. Can they elicit situations or visuals to represent a fact? Do they understand commutativity? Are they using flexible ways to find sums/products? Furthermore, journal writing is a *learning* activity. Students are increasing their understanding as they prepare their responses. Journal writing can also document mastery of fact sets or strategies, be used to show growth over time, and be shared with families to show their children's thinking.

Quizzes, Self-Assessments, and Progress Monitoring

The notion of a facts quiz may seem inconsistent with what we have already shown about timed testing, but there are genuinely effective ways to use written work samples or quizzes to measure students' progress toward fluency. First, *turn off the timers!* Removing the pressure of time allows students to solve problems in a low-stress environment, leading to more reliable measures of their accuracy and efficiency. Some students can count faster than they can determine whether a fact is a combination of 10 or a double. This is one reason why an emphasis on speed can impede progress toward mastery, particularly once derived fact strategies are added to the mix. When you draw attention to the fact that using a strategy is more valuable than counting, even if it takes more time initially, it encourages students to work on learning the foundational fact sets. Integrating self-monitoring and self-assessment prompts can make worksheets or quizzes helpful for students and teachers. Consider these five suggestions for using written work effectively.

Facts Quest

Key to fluency with foundational facts is recognizing one when you see it—in other words, spotting a known fact among a set of mixed facts. Facts quests allow you to repurpose old worksheets or timed tests that contain lots of mixed facts. One option is to have the students just find and circle the facts; another option is to have them find and solve the identified facts. For addition, for example, students can search for combinations of 10 or subtraction facts involving a combination of 10. For multiplication, students can search for all the squares and record answers. Fact quests can be adapted to each of the fact sets and eventually be used for *any and all* foundational facts.

Facts Check

It helps students to know that their basic fact experiences are intended to help them move away from counting to automaticity. Of course, we don't want students to be embarrassed about counting and hide it but rather to be open about moving to other ways to more efficiently determine the answer. Tell students that you are interested in the way they are solving facts so that you can support their progress toward mastery. Ask them to solve each problem on the facts check and share the way that they thought about it (see Figure 6.1). The figure only shows three facts, but a facts check could present as many as 10 and provide very useful data. (Note that this facts check could be used for multiplication, substituting the phrase "I skip counted" for "I counted.")

FIGURE 6.1   Sample Facts Check for Addition

Solve. Check the way you figured out each problem.

1. 4 + 4 = _____
   - ☐ I counted.
   - ☐ I used a strategy.
   - ☐ I just know.

2. 4 + 6 = _____
   - ☐ I counted.
   - ☐ I used a strategy.
   - ☐ I just know.

3. 3 + 5 = _____
   - ☐ I counted.
   - ☐ I used a strategy.
   - ☐ I just know.

To get more accurate responses about the strategies used, model for students how to decide which box to check. Although students may not know how they thought about finding the sum or product, that information in and of itself is an important finding. It means that more attention is needed to help students recognize the difference between counting, using a strategy, and just knowing. This helps students to self-monitor and see the progress they are making.

Self-Assess Automaticity

Explain that you want to know which facts the students just know or can say within a few seconds. Give out a page of 10–15 foundational facts and ask students to circle the ones they feel they could answer within three seconds. When finished, they invite you to see their paper, and you can ask them any of the circled facts to verify their assessment. (You can also ask ones that are not circled.)

Self-Reflect on Easy/Tough Facts

Give a list of about 15 foundational facts for students to answer. As students work, have them star the easier ones and circle the toughies (i.e., where they took more time or weren't sure what to do). Alternately, they can answer the facts first and then loop back to add stars and circles. This activity can also be done with a partner, sorting flash cards into two piles (easy and tough).

Facts Sort

Flash cards can serve a new purpose by inviting students to conduct a facts sort. Give each student a placemat, such as the one illustrated in Figure 6.2, use actual bowls, or just fold a paper into three sections and label it as the bowls are labeled.

Students place each fact into the appropriate bowl based on how they found it. As students are sorting the facts, they are getting the same amount of practice as a full worksheet, and you can pick up any card they have placed, and ask them to tell you the answer and explain how they solved it.

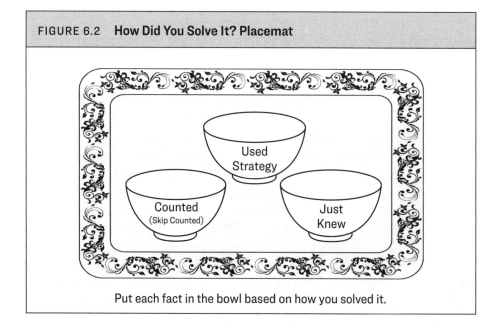

FIGURE 6.2   **How Did You Solve It? Placemat**

Used Strategy

Counted (Skip Counted)

Just Knew

Put each fact in the bowl based on how you solved it.

Charting Each Student's Fluency

Students progress through the three phases of fact fluency at different times for different groups of facts. However, before students can develop advanced fact strategies to solve the most difficult addition and subtraction facts, they must master the foundational facts. The same is true for multiplication and division. By using a variety of the assessments described in this chapter, a comprehensive picture of each student's progress toward mastering the foundational facts (Phase 3) can be obtained. Detailed progress toward mastery/automaticity on specific fact sets can be tracked using a copy of the flexible learning progression for each student. Simply laminate it (or place it in plastic) and use markers or sticky notes to record how individual students are doing with each set of facts across the year. An example for addition is provided in Figure 6.3. Once a student is making steady progress toward "Got it," you know it is time to start formally developing derived fact strategies.

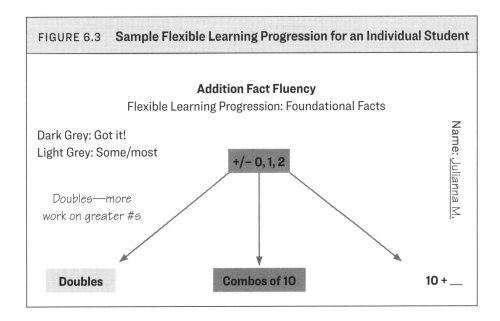

FIGURE 6.3   Sample Flexible Learning Progression for an Individual Student

Addition Fact Fluency

Flexible Learning Progression: Foundational Facts

Dark Grey: Got it!
Light Grey: Some/most

+/– 0, 1, 2

Doubles—more work on greater #s

Doubles

Combos of 10

10 + __

Name: Julianna M.

Instead of using the flexible learning progression, you may prefer to use a chart format, as shown in Tool 12. A chart like this can help you monitor student progress across the phases with the foundational facts (in this case, for multiplication).

TOOL 12

Foundational Facts Progress Chart for Multiplication

■ ■ ■ ■

Multiplication Progress Chart

Name: _____   Date: _____

Multiplication Foundational Fact Sets	Phase 1	Phase 2	Phase 3
	Uses skip counting	Recognizes commutative property; applies a strategy	Responds within three seconds *without* skip counting
2s			
10s			
5s			
1s			
0s			
Squares			

Summary

Monitoring students individually is extremely helpful for planning purposes. The assessment tools presented in this chapter can be used to determine which students need explicit strategy instruction, which games are going to be most helpful to which students, and what you might communicate to families to support students' progress toward mastering the foundational facts in addition or multiplication. When you see that most of your students are in Phase 3 for foundational facts, it is time to begin learning the derived fact strategies (see Chapters 3 and 5) and assessing progress with those facts. Assessing derived fact strategies is the focus of the next chapter.

7

Assessing Derived Fact Strategies and All Facts

Perhaps you've heard it in the teacher's lounge: "My kids just don't know their facts." Sadly, you may have heard it from a student: "I just can't learn my facts." In either case, a statement like this raises a few questions:

- Which facts are known? Which are not known?
- Which strategies does the student know, or is the student still counting?
- Is the student unable to get a correct answer or just not able to do it within three seconds?

These questions are best answered by using formative assessment tools. Observations, interviews, journals, and other tools can provide insights into what students know, what strategies make sense to them, and what their next learning opportunities need to be.

The five fundamentals also connect to the material presented in this chapter.

1. **Mastery must focus on fluency**. The four components of fluency can only be assessed through formative assessment tools. Some students can become fast counters (or skip counters); others can become overly reliant on a single strategy. Flexibility and strategy selection must be monitored carefully.

2. **Fluency develops in three phases.** This chapter assumes that students have mastered the foundational facts and focuses on monitoring students' progress to Phase 3 for all facts (within 20 for addition and within 100 for multiplication).

3. **Foundational facts must precede derived facts.** If assessments indicate a lack of automaticity with one or more foundational fact sets, we suggest returning to the practice and assessments outlined in Chapters 2 and 6 (addition) or Chapters 4 and 6 (multiplication).

4. **Timed tests do not assess fluency.** We must monitor which facts students know and what strategies they are using to ensure that each student masters all facts. Timed tests cannot provide this information, so why subject students to these stress-inducing assessments?

5. **Students need substantial and enjoyable practice.** We share many assessments that are effective in gathering data, often as students are engaged in practice.

Before we begin, let's revisit Fundamental 2: Fluency develops in three phases. These are reviewed in more detail below as they relate to assessment goals. The questions for each phase must be answered to support students' progress toward mastery. A review of these questions only reinforces how inadequate timed tests are for assessing students; timed tests just don't provide the data that are needed to monitor which facts and strategies students know and which they need to revisit or learn.

Phase 1: Counting

- Is the student counting/skip counting?
- For what types of problems is the student counting/skip counting?

Phase 2: Deriving

- Does the student know the foundational facts?
- Is the student able to use a derived fact strategy?
- Is the student choosing an efficient strategy for the problem at hand?
- Which derived fact strategies is the student using, and for which problem types?

Phase 3: Mastery

- Is the student able to implement a particular strategy *efficiently?*
- For which facts is the student producing correct responses within three seconds? (Which facts/fact sets need more instruction or practice?)

This chapter assumes that students have mastered the foundational facts and provides ideas and tools for assessing the development of the derived fact strategies. If you are not sure whether your students know the foundational facts, use one of the observation or interview protocols from Chapter 6. This chapter provides tools for assessing derived facts, each of which are easily adapted to focus on other sets of derived facts; for example, assessment tools for addition can be adapted to multiplication, subtraction, or division.

Observations

When students are learning foundational facts, they are focusing on very specific facts within particular categories. However, when they move into derived facts, *any* of the derived fact strategies can be used. For example, for an addition fact such as 6 + 8, a student may choose from the Near Doubles, Making 10, or Pretend-a-10 strategies. A multiplication fact such as 7 × 9 might be solved by Subtracting a Group or the Break Apart strategy. Therefore, students need think time to ask themselves questions such as, *Which strategy do I want to use? How will I break apart the numbers?* Games play a central role when it comes to derived fact strategies, which is why we include more than 40 games in this book. Games provide the opportunity to (1) practice one of the derived fact strategies, (2) practice choosing from among the strategies or decide how to break apart an addend/factor, and (3) become accurate and automatic in applying strategies (or just knowing the facts). We use these three possibilities to organize some sample observation tools.

As with the foundational facts, we begin with three questions that will help you determine your observation tool. Once you reflect on these three questions, the tool can be selected or created.

- Which set(s) of facts or strategies are you assessing?
- What components of fluency are you addressing?
- Are you assessing automaticity/mastery?

Addition Derived Fact Strategies

Let's first look at Making 10 as the strategy selected. Chapter 3 outlined the thinking involved in this strategy; Figure 7.1 adds specific understandings behind the thinking that a teacher needs to assess.

FIGURE 7.1	**Analysis of Making 10 Strategy Reasoning**	
Mental Process in Symbols	**What Students Might Think or Say as They Solve**	**What Students Must Know (Diagnostic Analysis)**
8 + 7 = __	Eight is 2 away from 10. I will use the Making 10 strategy and move 2 over from the 7.	Missing addend version of combinations of 10: 8 + __ = 10
8 + 2 + __ = ?	If I break apart 7 into 2 and some more, what is left?	How to decompose 7: 7 = 2 + 5 OR Know subtraction within 10 7 − 2 = 5
8 + 2 + 5 = ?	Now I make 10 (add 8 and 2) and then add on the 5.	Knows 10 + __ facts: 10 + 5 = 15
10 + 5 = 15	I know 10 + 5 equals 15.	

An observation tool, therefore, might be focused on diagnosing if a student has the component skills to use the strategy. You can use a chart like the one shown in Tool 13 and write a simple *Yes* or *No* or make a check mark for each of the skills as you watch students play a game and describe this strategy, or as you show them a fact and ask them to think aloud through the Making 10 strategy. Notes can be recorded to help guide your instruction. For example, a student might be very successful with the Making 10 strategy when one of the addends is a 9 but not able to use the strategy for a problem like 6 + 8.

A similar tool can be created for each of the other addition derived fact strategies. The thinking processes for each of those strategies are described in Figure 7.2.

Multiplication Derived Fact Strategies

Adding a Group is a highly useful derived fact strategy for multiplication and requires automaticity with 1s, 2s, and 5s. Observations, therefore, are needed to verify both automaticity with foundational facts and the student's ability to decompose the original fact to apply these foundational facts (see Chapter 5 for elaboration). Figure 7.3 adds considerations for assessment.

TOOL 13

Observation Tool for the
Making 10 Strategy

■ ■ ■ ■

Names	Making 10 Strategy Components			Notes
	Knows missing number to make a combo of 10	Can decompose other addend	Can add the remaining part to 10	Which facts? How efficient?

As this thought process illustrates, there are several elements that a student must know and be able to do to "own" this strategy. An observation tool can document these elements, providing the essential data to diagnose what a student needs to use the strategy effectively. The example provided in Figure 7.3 not only applies to Adding a Group but to any of the derived fact strategies because they are all based on decomposing or changing one of the factors. Tool 14 provides a generic observation tool that can be used for any multiplication derived fact strategy.

Selection of Strategies

The key to fluency is selecting an efficient strategy. Determining which strategy is efficient depends on the numbers in the fact. Compare, for example, 9 + 1 and 9 + 8.

Counting on is an efficient strategy for the first fact but not for the second. The fact 9×6 can be found efficiently using any of these strategies:

FIGURE 7.2	**Analysis of Near Doubles and Pretend-a-10 Reasoning**	
Mental Process in Symbols	**What Students Might Think or Say as They Solve**	**What Students Must Know (Diagnostic Analysis)**
Near Doubles		
9 + 8 = __	These numbers are close to each other, so I can use a double.	Recognize choices (8 + 8 or 9 + 9)
(8 + 1) + 8 = __	I will break apart 9 into 8 and 1. Then I have double 8 and one more.	How to break apart 9 as 8 + 1 or know *one less* subtraction fact: 9 − 1 = 8
8 + 8 + 1 = __	I know 8 + 8. It is 16.	Doubles fact: 8 + 8 = 16
16 + 1 = 17	One more than 16 is 17.	*One more* facts for numbers between 10 and 20
Pretend-a-10		
8 + 7 = __	I am going to pretend the 8 is a 10.	Recognize proximity of 8 to 10
8 10 + 7 = __	I know my 10 + __ facts. This equals 17.	Know 10 + __ facts: 10 + 7
10 + 7 = 17	I have to adjust my answer. Eight is 2 away from 10, so I need to take 2 away from 17.	Missing addend version of combinations of 10: 8 + __ = 10
17 − 2 = 15	Two less than 17 is 15.	Know *two less* facts between 10 and 20

- **Subtracting a Group.** Notice that 9 is one group less than 10: $10 \times 6 - 6 = 60 - 6 = 54$
- **Adding a Group.** Notice that 6 is one group more than 5: $9 \times 5 + 9 = 45 + 9 = 54$
- **Doubling.** If 3s facts are known, decompose 6: $(9 \times 3) \times 2 = 27 \times 2 = 54$

For derived fact sets, there are almost always several good choices for efficient strategies. Observation tools can also be used to focus on whether students are selecting an efficient strategy and if they are picking a variety of strategies across problems. Examples for addition, subtraction, and multiplication are provided in Tool 15. (Division is not included because there is really only one strategy—Think Multiplication.)

FIGURE 7.3	**Analysis of Adding a Group Reasoning**	
Mental Process in Symbols	**What Students Might Think or Say as They Solve**	**What Students Must Know (Diagnostic Analysis)**
$6 \times 8 =$ __?	I see 6 and know that it is one more than 5.	Notice that because there is a factor of 6 they can break apart into 5s and 1s facts.
$5 \times 8 + 1 \times 8 =$ __?	I break apart 6 to have 5 groups of 8 and one more group of 8.	6 is one more *group* of 8, not just one more.
$40 + 8 =$ __?	I multiply 5×8. I know this is 40.	5s facts.
48	I add one more 8 to 40 and it equals 48.	To add 8 (and not 1).

These observation tools are very flexible in terms of what is recorded within the cells. Options for this type of observation chart include the following:

- **Frequency of selection (flexibility, strategy selection).** Tally each time the strategy is appropriately chosen.

- **Effective use of strategy (accuracy/efficiency).** Use a check mark for using a strategy accurately or a star for being accurate *and* automatic.
- **Specific facts/fact sets (strategy selection/automaticity).** Record the facts for which the student uses each strategy. For example, if a student uses Near Doubles to solve 9 + 8, write "9 + 8" in the Near Doubles column. Add a star if it is given within three seconds.

TOOL 14

Observation Tool for Any Multiplication Derived Fact Strategy ■ ■ ■ ■

Names	Strategy Components				Notes
	Recognizes factor that "fits" the strategy	Can decompose or change factor	Has automaticity with foundational facts used	Combines partial products or adjusts accurately and efficiently	Which fact sets? How efficient?

As you are listening to students think aloud as they play games, you will hear and see them solve various facts. As you record their strategy selections, you will get a sense of which ones they choose and whether they can appropriately apply them. A student may master the facts without using some of the specific derived fact strategies shared in this book. For example, a student may just not "need" Near Doubles or Near Squares because they prefer to use other strategies. However, they need to be able to use strategies proficiently enough to solve derived fact sets efficiently and flexibly, without resorting to counting.

TOOL 15

Observation Tools for Selection of Strategies

■   ■   ■   ■

Names	Addition Strategy Selected				
	Foundational Fact (known)	Near Doubles	Making 10	Pretend-a-10	Other

Names	Subtraction Strategy Selected				
	Counting Up/Back	Think Addition	Down over 10	Up over 10	Take from 10

Names	Multiplication Strategy Selected						
	Founda-tional Fact (known)	Doubling	Adding a Group	Sub-tracting a Group	Near Square	Break Apart	Other (e.g., Skip Count-ing)

Your observation tool tells a story about each student's thinking. For example, you may see a small group of students find 3 + 4, 6 + 7, and 9 + 8. One student might use Near Doubles for all three facts, while another student might just know 3 + 4, use Near Doubles for 6 + 7, and use Pretend-a-10 for 9 + 8. What does this tell you about these students? You know that the first student can apply Near Doubles (Phase 2), and you will be able to determine if she can apply it within three seconds (Phase 3). However, you do not know if she has developed additional strategies. You might continue to listen to see what other cards are drawn, or you might just lean in and ask the student, "How would you solve 4 + 8?," as this fact is more efficiently solved by Making 10 or Pretend-a-10. You can see that the second student can select appropriate strategies and demonstrate flexibility. Based on whether she has answered the question correctly and how easily she found it, you also know her accuracy and efficiency. In other words, through observation, you can assess all four components of fluency!

As you use the observation tools given in this chapter, keep in mind that initial recording should *not* focus on automaticity with all facts. This is a goal for the *end* of the year (typically the end of 2nd grade for addition and end of 3rd or 4th grade for multiplication). In many state standards, automaticity is not an expectation for subtraction or division at all, although using a strategy other than counting/skip counting is a goal. It takes a significant number of opportunities practicing the strategies, both choosing and using them, before students can think through these processes quickly or come to "just know" the facts. We have stated the following several times in this book, but it is worth repeating: Do not push for speed too soon; time pressure often pushes students back to counting strategies, working against your efforts for students to adopt strategies that will eventually be more efficient.

Accuracy and Automaticity

Students will progress through the three phases of mastery for different facts at different times of the year. It is not surprising to find a single student in all three phases at the same time, depending on the fact set selected. When observing for mastery, you may prefer a very specific observation tool to determine which students have automaticity and accuracy with a particular fact set, and you may also include strategy selection. Although these detailed lists could include any fact sets for addition, subtraction, multiplication, or division, in this section we will focus on a subset that we refer to as the toughies—the facts that tend to be hardest for students to master and for which they benefit greatly from learning and practicing a derived fact strategy.

Tool 16 lists several addition facts that generally require a derived fact strategy. Keep in mind that, for simplicity, the table assumes students understand commutativity, for example, recognizing that 4 + 9 = 9 + 4.

TOOL 16

Observation Tool for Strategies and Mastery for Addition Facts   ■ ■ ■ ■

Names	Facts Between 11 and 17, Excluding Foundational Facts														
	3 + 8	3 + 9	4 + 7	4 + 8	4 + 9	5 + 6	5 + 7	5 + 8	5 + 9	6 + 7	6 + 8	6 + 9	7 + 8	7 + 9	8 + 9

Code: I = Inefficient method used (e.g., counting when it is not a +1, +2 situation)

S = (Efficient) strategy used (e.g., Pretend-a-10)

K = Just knew (recall)

* = Automatic (fact given in three seconds or less)

For multiplication, the foundational facts cover *most* of the facts in the multiplication table. If you assume students can apply the commutative property of multiplication, the list is further shortened. The remaining facts tend to be the toughies for multiplication; they are included in the observation tool in Tool 17.

The beauty of these observation tools is that you can see for which facts a student is using inefficient approaches, as well as which strategies they can use. This information can help to identify reteaching or practice activities.

TOOL 17

Observation Tool for Strategies and Mastery for Multiplication Facts   ■ ■ ■ ■

Names	Multiplication Facts That Are Not Foundational Facts													
	4 × 3	6 × 3	7 × 3	8 × 3	9 × 3	6 × 4	7 × 4	8 × 4	9 × 4	7 × 6	8 × 6	9 × 6	8 × 7	9 × 7	9 × 8

Code: I = Inefficient method used (e.g., Skip Counting)

S = (Efficient) strategy used (e.g., Adding a Group or Break Apart)

K = Just knew (recall)

* = Automatic (fact given in three seconds or less)

Interviewing

As described in Chapter 6, interviewing is a highly effective technique for assessing the components of fluency as well as automaticity. With derived fact strategies, interviews are *even more critical*, as there are more choices and steps involved in finding the answer.

In-the-Moment Interviews

Because students need a lot of practice choosing and applying strategies, this assessment technique is very practical and informative when used in a game setting. Simply ask, "Did you use a strategy? Which strategy did you use?" This provides important insights about whether students know how to use a strategy, encourages students to articulate their thinking, and, if asked during game play, exposes other students to a variety of ways to find the answer. Tool 18 provides a guide for assessing each component of fluency through interviewing during game play. Recall from the discussion in Chapter 1 on fluency that appropriate strategy selection is required for both efficiency and flexibility, so it is represented within both of those categories, rather than separately.

TOOL 18

Interview Prompts for Assessing Fluency During Game Play   ■ ■ ■ ■

As Students Play a Basic Facts Game ...	
Accuracy	• Listen and watch. Are they getting correct answers? • Ask, "What answer did you get?"
Efficiency and strategy selection	• Silently count as students play to assess time taken to answer. Are they applying the strategy in a reasonable time frame? • Ask, "How did you solve it?" • Ask, "Was it an efficient strategy?"
Flexibility and strategy selection	• Listen and watch. Are they using different strategies for different fact sets? • Ask, "Why did you pick that strategy?" • Ask, "Is there another strategy that you could use for that problem?" • Ask, "When do you use _____ strategy instead of _____ strategy?

If you notice that students are struggling to remember all options for derived fact strategies, create a class poster or bulletin board that lists and illustrates the strategies. Additionally, having a strategy list in hand can help. Invite students to create their own lists and put strategies in priority order, based on which ones they like to use the most.

One-on-One Interviews: Choosing a Strategy

Selecting from among strategies is central to fluency and to mastery of basic facts. There are at least two ways to interview students and get a sense of how they are doing with selecting an efficient strategy. First, you can simply ask for answers to given facts that lend themselves to multiple appropriate fact strategies, such as the following Four Facts Interview Protocols:

Addition:
- 6 + 7
- 8 + 7
- 9 + 5
- 7 + 5

Subtraction:
- 17 − 9
- 12 − 4
- 11 − 2
- 15 − 6

Multiplication:
- 7 × 4
- 6 × 8
- 9 × 7
- 9 × 8

After hearing and observing as students answer all four facts, you can pose follow-up questions (such as those in Tool 19) based on how they applied strategies.

A second way that you can effectively assess students on strategy selection is to have students sort a small stack of fact cards based on how they would solve them. (A similar activity was presented in Chapter 6 for the foundational facts.) Figure 7.4 shows simple placemats that you can make for the sorting activity, or you can use actual bowls or a folded piece of paper with labeled sections. The placemats in the figure highlight addition and multiplication strategies, but a placemat for subtraction could be made as well (Counting Up/Back, Think Addition, Using 10, Just Know, and Other). This interview can also be done with a small group of students, having them rotate to a strategy sort station in the classroom during game time.

TOOL 19

Four Facts Protocol Follow-Up Interview Questions   ■ ■ ■ ■

What You Hear or Observe	To Conclude the Interview, Say
Student uses two or three strategies, answering each fairly quickly. (Interpretation: student is selecting and using strategies flexibly and efficiently.)	"I noticed you used several strategies. How do you decide which one to use?"
Student uses one strategy, answering each fact fairly quickly. (Interpretation: student is selecting and using a single strategy efficiently across the set.)	"I noticed you solved these efficiently with the _____ strategy. Why did you pick that one? Is there another strategy that would work for these problems?"
Student uses the same strategy for all facts but gets stuck on some of them. (Interpretation: student is using one strategy but may not know, or may not think to try, other strategies.)	"I noticed you using the _____ strategy for the first few problems, but then you got stuck. Is there another strategy that might be a good match?"

As you are observing, the student flips over a fact card, says the answer, and places it in the appropriate "bowl." As they work, you can also check automaticity by noting how much time it takes the student to answer. When the student has finished sorting, you can do a strategy share. Select one card from a strategy bowl and ask the student to talk you through the thinking process. If the strategy matches the thinking, leave the card in the bowl. If the strategy doesn't match, together determine where it should be moved. If all the cards end up in the Just Know bowl, ask the student to share how they would help a student who *doesn't* know that fact to use a reasoning strategy to find the answer.

It is not important that every student can use every strategy. A student who has placed all the addition fact cards in the Just Know and Making 10 bowls and is generating answers easily, for example, does not necessarily need explicit instruction on Near Doubles or Pretend-a-10. The goal is not to master the reasoning strategies but to use the reasoning strategies to master the facts. This is true for all the operations. That being said, if there are facts that are difficult for a student, revisiting one of the reasoning strategies and practicing it meaningfully could be the best route to obtaining mastery of those facts.

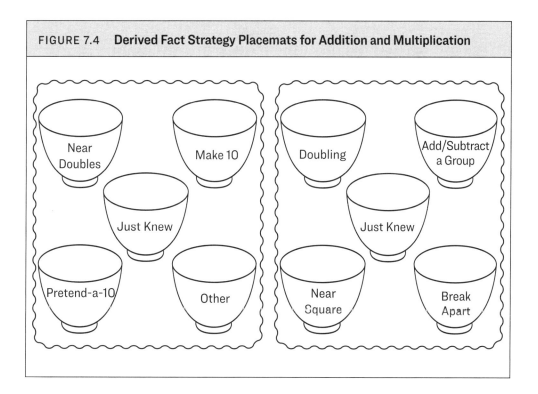

FIGURE 7.4   Derived Fact Strategy Placemats for Addition and Multiplication

One-on-One Interviews: Mastery and Fluency

Ultimately, teachers, parents, administrators, and other stakeholders want to know, "Has each student mastered all the basic facts?" The timed test has traditionally been used to make this determination, despite evidence that the stress students experience results in it being a poor measure of what they actually know. Although a single interview should not include every fact, it is possible to ascertain through several interviews whether a student has mastered all the basic addition or multiplication facts. As described in Chapter 6, using a formal interview to determine fluency or mastery takes more time and careful documentation, so plans must be put into place—ideally with some assistance, perhaps from a mathematics specialist or teaching assistant. Tool 20 provides two options for addition facts, one focused on mastery only and one focused on both mastery and fluency. These interviews might be implemented at strategic points during the year to see how a student is progressing toward mastery (Phase 3).

Tool 21 provides parallel tools for multiplication facts. Either of these tools can be used at checkpoints throughout 2nd grade and at the beginning of 3rd grade (or any grade in which students may not have automaticity with addition facts).

You can decide to designate that the student used a strategy (with an S), or you can use the suggested codes for recording specific strategies that were applied. The former is simpler, but the latter gives more data on flexibility and strategy selection.

TOOL 20

Student Records for Addition   ■   ■   ■   ■

Addition Mastery Record
Instructions: Have facts ready on cards or a screen. Show one at a time. If student takes more time to respond, skip some of the facts. Use a *silent* count for automaticity. Record appropriate code next to each fact.

Student:	Date:

Possible facts to show (assumes commutativity; be sure the greater addend is sometimes first and sometimes last)

9 + 3	9 + 9	6 + 7	3 + 8	7 + 9	5 + 8
8 + 4	5 + 3	7 + 7	7 + 4	5 + 6	6 + 8

✓ = Accuracy (correct but required more than three seconds)
* = Automaticity (accurate response within three seconds)

Addition Fluency Record											

Instructions: Have facts ready on cards or a screen. Show one at a time. If student takes more time to respond, skip some of the facts. Use a *silent* count for automaticity. For each, wait for an answer, then ask, "How did you solve it?" Record appropriate code next to each fact.

Possible facts to show (assumes commutativity; be sure the greater addend is sometimes first and sometimes last)

7 + 6		9 + 3		7 + 8		5 + 7		6 + 9		8 + 4	

Mastery Codes (record in space below each fact)
X = Mastery
✓ = Accurate (correct but required more than three seconds)
* = Automatic (accurate response within three seconds)

Strategy Codes (record in space **to the right** of each fact as student explains)
C= Count on
S = Strategy   **ND**= Near Doubles   **M10**= Making 10   **P10** = Pretend-a-10
K = Just knew (recall)

Because the fluency records provide specific data on which strategies students can and cannot use, they are highly effective formative assessment tools. Results will help you to select instructional next steps (quick looks and games) that can address any facts or strategies that need more explicit instruction. Beyond using these tools as formal assessments to track students' mastery, they can be used for diagnosis and remediation for students who have not yet mastered the facts. In addition, they can be adapted for use with subtraction and division facts.

As the end of the year approaches, you may need an assessment to determine whether students have reached the goal of automaticity for addition or multiplication facts and are using efficient strategies (beyond counting) for subtraction and division facts. Tool 22 provides an example of an exit interview for addition facts. This interview focuses on the derived facts, assuming automaticity with the foundational

TOOL 21

Student Records for Multiplication

■ ■ ■ ■

Multiplication Mastery Record
Instructions: Have facts ready on cards or a screen. Show one at a time. If student takes more time to respond, skip some of the facts. Use a *silent* count for automaticity. Record appropriate code next to each fact.

Student:	Date:

Possible facts to show (assumes commutativity; be sure the greater multiplicand is sometimes first and sometimes last)

5 × 3	8 × 2	4 × 7	3 × 8	6 × 8	9 × 8
8 × 4	9 × 3	7 × 7	6 × 5	9 × 6	7 × 8

✓ = Accurate (correct but required more than three seconds)
* = Automatic (accurate response within three seconds)

Multiplication Fluency Record
Instructions: Have facts ready on cards or a screen. Show one at a time. For each, wait for an answer, then ask, "How did you solve it?" Record appropriate code next to each fact.

Possible facts to show (assumes commutativity; be sure the greater multiplicand is sometimes first and sometimes last)

4 × 6		6 × 7		7 × 8		8 × 4		6 × 9		9 × 3	

Mastery Codes (record in space below each fact)
✓ = Accuracy (correct but required more than three seconds)
* = Automaticity (accurate response within three seconds)

Strategy Codes (record in space **to the right** of each fact as student explains)
C= Skip Counts
S = Strategy   **D**= Doubling   **G**= Adding/Subtracting a Group
NS = Near Squares   **BA** = Break Apart   **O** = Other
K = Just knew (recall)

facts, and includes the toughies, many of which can be solved by using any of the derived fact strategies. It is important to note that a student can be so fast at using these strategies that it is difficult to distinguish between using a strategy and just knowing the fact without probing for how they figured it out. But this distinction may not be needed because students just need to answer within three seconds to be considered automatic.

TOOL 22

Exit Interview for Addition Facts ■ ■ ■ ■

Exit Interview: Addition Facts		
Name:	**Date:**	
Instructions: Say or show each fact to the student. Silently count as they think of their answer. Record the code next to the fact. Code: A = Accurate, E = Efficient strategy used, * = Automatic		
1. 8 + 6 _____ 2. 7 + 5 _____ 3. 9 + 8 _____ 4. 4 + 8 _____ 5. 6 + 9 _____ 6. 8 + 3 _____ 7. 6 + 7 _____ 8. 5 + 8 _____	9, 7 + 7 10. 5 + 6 _____ 11. 9 + 7 _____ 12. 5 + 4 _____ 13. 8 + 7 _____ 14. 5 + 9 _____ 15. 4 + 6 _____	
Notes:		

The exit assessment in Tool 22 can be adapted to multiplication simply by changing the fact set, being sure to include most of the toughies. Notes may include comments such as which strategy students commonly use, if they refer to visual models, and so on. An exit assessment can be used for subtraction and division as well, with the removal of the automaticity codes.

Scoring Interviews

Rather than codes, you may need numerical scores to communicate to stakeholders how students are performing and progressing toward basic fact mastery. Quite simply, you can determine an accuracy score and an automaticity score by calculating totals or percentages from the recording page. This is appropriate at the culmination of fact work when mastery is expected. Prior to that, to keep the focus on fluency, you will also want to score strategy selection and flexibility. Here are some suggestions for how you might score these.

Strategy selection. Count any *appropriate* strategy (i.e., not counting on, unless the sum is a +1 or +2, and not skip counting), as well as known facts, and give a strategy score. For example, suppose a student is asked to find eight different multiplication facts at the end of the year and can answer all the facts correctly (100 percent accuracy). If the student used skip counting on two out of the eight questions, used Break Apart for four items, and just knew two items, he or she would have 6/8 on strategy selection, or 75 percent.

Flexibility. Flexibility involves being able to select and use an appropriate strategy, and over a set of problems, these strategies will then vary. Therefore, this fluency component is harder to score. A holistic scoring guide or rubric, such as the one shown in Tool 23, can describe each student's progress toward fluency of all facts. Note that the scores of 3 and 4 include the use of different strategies, and therefore capture flexibility.

On this rubric, you may notice that there is a big leap between a score of 2 and a score of 3. In a four-point rubric, it is convenient and helpful to consider the two options to the left as "not there yet" and the two options to the right as "almost got it" or "got it!" Students scoring a 3 or 4 will benefit from ongoing practice through games and discussions but likely do not need explicit strategy instruction. Students scoring 1 or 2, however, need opportunities for explicit strategy instruction. This may include quick looks (ten frames for addition and equal groups for multiplication) and games focused on a specific strategy or that involve visuals (ten frames or arrays). Although a score alone does not provide the diagnostic and useful information that is captured on the actual recording sheet, it does provide an at-a-glance sense of the student's progress toward fluency and mastery (automaticity).

TOOL 23

Holistic Rubric for Basic Fact Fluency

■   ■   ■   ■

1	2	3	4
Knows some foundational facts but counts or skip counts for derived facts	Demonstrates automaticity with all foundational fact sets and uses at least one of the derived fact strategies for other facts	Demonstrates automaticity with all foundational fact sets and uses several derived fact strategies for most or all other facts, though may require processing time to implement some strategies	Demonstrates automaticity with all or most facts, selects efficient strategies and implements them easily, or just knows the facts

Journal Writing

Journal writing provides a way for students to demonstrate fact strategies using pictures, words, and number sentences, as well as an additional way for you to analyze their thinking. Writing is truly an example of assessment for learning, as students gain new insights as they organize their thoughts to prepare a journal entry. As needed, encourage students to use visuals, such as number lines and ten frames, to support their explanations. Tool 24 offers sample journal prompts for the operations for each aspect of fluency.

TOOL 24

A Dozen Writing Prompts
for Basic Fact Fluency

■ ■ ■ ■

Fluency Component	Sample Writing Prompts
Accuracy	Emily says 8 + 7 equals 15. Is she correct? How do you know?
	Danielle solved 6 × 9 by starting with 5 × 9 (45) and then adding on 1 more to equal 46. Is she correct? Explain why or why not.
Efficiency (including strategy selection)	Sydni solved 12 − 9 on a number line. She started at 12 and counted back 9. Is this efficient? If yes, tell why. If no, explain or show a good way to solve it.
	Is skip counting by 7s a good way to solve 6 × 7? If yes, tell why. If no, share a strategy that you think is better.
	Isaiah solved 72 ÷ 9 by deciding the answer had to be greater than 7, and so thought about 8 × 9. He multiplied 8 × 10 and subtracted 8 to confirm that 8 × 9 = 72. Is this a good way to solve this problem? If yes, tell why. If no, explain or show a good way to solve it.
	What strategy would you use for 16 − 7?
Strategy use	Hannah solved 6 + 9 by pretending the 9 was a 10 and adding 6 to 10 to get 16. Then she took one away to get 15. Is this a good strategy? If yes, tell why. If no, explain or show a good way to solve it.
	Olivia is stuck on the fact 9 × 7. You notice she is skip counting. Select a strategy and show or explain it so that Olivia will understand.
	Explain or show at least one way you can use Near Doubles to solve 7 + 8 (or Near Squares to solve 7 × 6).
Flexibility	How might you solve 8 × 7? List as many different strategies as you can. Then explain which one is your favorite and why.
	Would you solve these two problems the same way? Explain why or why not. 12 − 1 12 − 9
	Peter says, "I don't know *when* to use the Pretend-a-10 strategy." What would you say back to Peter?

A lot can be learned from these journal prompts. Four student responses to the question, "How many ways can you find 8 × 7?" are provided in Figure 7.5. Evaluate each response and determine whether you think the student demonstrates fluency (at least with this fact).

Some students struggle with writing and may need support in expressing their ideas. Sentence starters and strategy lists can help. For example, for the first three prompts in the Efficiency section in Tool 24, you can provide the following starters:

- I think this is a good strategy because _____.
- I do not think this strategy is helpful because _____. Instead, use _____ strategy. Here is how: _____.

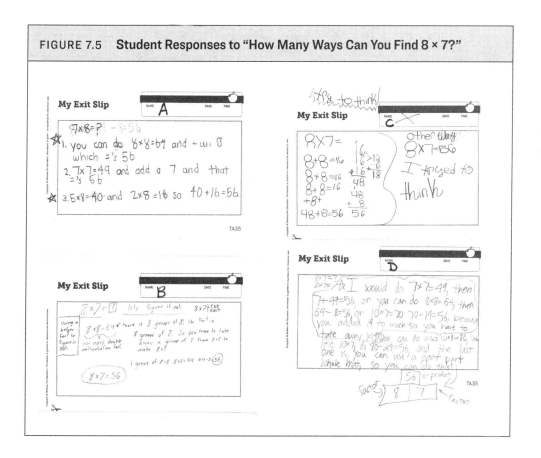

FIGURE 7.5   Student Responses to "How Many Ways Can You Find 8 × 7?"

Journal prompts can also be used to self-monitor and reflect. For example, after playing a game, you might ask students to think of one fact that was very easy for them as they played and one fact that took them more time. In their journal they can write:

- This fact was easy for me: _____. The strategy I used for this fact is: _____.
- This fact was tough for me: _____. A strategy I tried was _____. To get better at this fact, I will _____.

Sharing students' responses to these prompts with parents can help families focus attention on the facts their children find difficult. Once students have completed these prompts at school, they can also do them at home. Consider sending a game home to play as part of math homework. Ask families to play the game for 10–15 minutes and then complete these prompts with their child.

Self-Assessment and Strategy Quizzes

Many ideas for quizzes and self-assessments are described in Chapter 6 and can be readily adapted to derived facts. Remember, though—no timers! Focus on self-monitoring and self-assessment through activities such as these.

Strategy Quest

Give students a traditional mastery practice page or fact quiz. Have them select crayons or markers in three different colors. With the first color, the students circle all the facts they could solve using one strategy (e.g., Making 10 or Doubling). With the next color, they identify all the facts that can be found using a different strategy (e.g., Near Doubles or Adding/Subtracting a Group). Continue with the third color for another strategy. This activity works for subtraction, for example, by including the Counting Up/Back, Think Addition, and Using 10 strategies.

For follow-up discussion, look for a fact that the students have coded differently and use it for a number talk.

Strategy Check

Remove all but one column from a quiz or worksheet; alternately, limit the quiz to about 10 items. Insert a strategy checklist, as illustrated in Figure 7.6, or have students just write in their strategy. Upon completion, students can look at which strategies they used and which ones they didn't, reflecting on why this might be the case.

The example provided is for multiplication, but the same idea works for addition and subtraction facts.

FIGURE 7.6	**Strategy Check: Derived Multiplication Facts**
Fact Check: All Multiplication Facts Solve. Show how you figured it out. Check the way you thought about each problem.	
1. 6 × 3 = _____	☐ I skip counted. ☐ I used _____ strategy. ☐ I just knew.
2. 8 × 4 = _____	☐ I skip counted. ☐ I used _____ strategy. ☐ I just knew.
3. 9 × 6 = _____	☐ I skip counted. ☐ I used _____ strategy. ☐ I just knew.
4. 8 × 7 = _____	☐ I skip counted. ☐ I used _____ strategy. ☐ I just knew.
5. 7 × 6 =	☐ I skip counted. ☐ I used _____ strategy. ☐ I just knew.

Self-Assess Automaticity

As in the strategy quest, students circle the facts they feel they knew within three seconds (see the example for addition in Figure 7.7). They can circle the facts after having recorded an answer, or they can circle them without recording an answer; then you can ask a fact from the ones they have circled.

Self-Reflect on Easy/Tough Facts

This can be used for any operation. With the students, define an *easy* fact as one where they know an efficient strategy or can recall the answer without counting/skip counting, and a *tough* fact as one where they need to count/skip count or take a lot of time to select or use a strategy. Students can code the facts on a worksheet or quiz as *E* or *T*. Alternately, a partner can hold flash cards for the student and then place the automatic ones in one pile and the ones that take more think time in another pile. After each partner has a turn, they can look at their toughies and think about which strategies they might use next time to solve them more efficiently. (This could also be an interview or journal writing task.)

FIGURE 7.7   Sample "I Just Know It!" Quiz

Circle all the facts where you know the answer automatically.

1. $7 + 9 =$ _____
2. $4 + 3 =$ _____
3. $9 + 8 =$ _____
4. $6 + 5 =$ _____
5. $6 + 9 =$ _____
6. $8 + 2 =$ _____
7. $7 + 8 =$ _____
8. $10 + 8 =$ _____
9. $7 + 6 =$ _____
10. $5 + 4 =$ _____

What do you notice about the facts you know automatically?

Strategy Sort

Although presented as an interview technique earlier in this chapter, another way to infuse self-reflection into traditional practice or tests is to invite students to use the placemats illustrated in Figure 7.4. Students cut out all the facts on a worksheet, and then select one from the pile, record their answer, and place it on the appropriate bowl based on how they thought about it. After the students complete their stacks, they can tape or glue their answers down. Beyond being a rich source of insight into the student's thinking, this placemat can be used for instructional purposes. For example, students can be asked to compare their placemats with a friend, finding one fact they solved the same way and one fact they solved differently. The students then explain to each other the different strategies. Next, they move to new partners to repeat the process. At the end of this mixer, the class can reflect on which strategies they or their friends are using frequently, which strategies are less common, and which strategies they have as strengths or need to work on.

Charting Each Student's Basic Fact Mastery

If you are teaching in a grade that requires mastery of facts, then the full flexible learning progression can be copied and laminated for each student (see Figures 1.2 and 1.3). You can use these progressions for documentation throughout the year and for discussions with parents about their child's progress (see Figure 6.3 for an example). This layout communicates to parents the developmental nature of fact fluency, helping them to see where they can provide support more effectively. Furthermore, it is a great tool for helping students monitor their own progress toward mastery. This same information could also be recorded in a chart, such as the one illustrated in Tool 25 for addition facts. You may even wish to record the month, or use different colors for each marking period, to track more specifically when students progressed to the next phase.

Tool 25 can be adapted for assessment with multiplication facts as well, or you might use the comprehensive record provided in Tool 26. You can simply make check marks in the cells, or you can record specific facts that fall in each phase, which can be noted for follow-up.

Summary

Recall that we began this chapter by asking what it means when someone says, "My students don't know their facts." Using the tools presented in this chapter allows us to instead say, "This student knows *these* facts with automaticity, can use *these* strategies (with or without automaticity), and is now working on *these* facts or strategies." In this way, instruction can be focused on exactly what each student needs to master the basic facts. After all, isn't that the goal of assessment? This is the kind of information that is important to share with families about their child. Of course, they will need to understand why it is important for their child to be learning reasoning strategies and why you are teaching and assessing basic facts the way that you are. Chapter 8 provides ideas for helping families understand, embrace, and support your basic fact fluency plan.

TOOL 25

Progress Monitoring Tool for Addition Facts

■   ■   ■   ■

Name:						
Foundational Facts						
	Phase 1			**Phase 2**		**Phase 3**
Fact Subset	Counts all	Counts on from first number	Counts on from greater number	Recognizes the fact set ("This is a double.")	Can use fact set to add/subtract	Solves problems quickly (within three seconds)
Sums involving +0, +1, or +2						
Doubles						
Combinations of 10						
10 + ___						
Derived Fact Strategies						
	Phase 1		**Phase 2**		**Phase 3**	
Fact Subset	Counts		Can use strategy when asked	Chooses an efficient strategy	Solves problems quickly (within three seconds)	
Sums with an addend of 7, 8 or 9* (e.g., 8 + 3, 9 + 7)						

Sums with close addends** (e.g., 5 + 7; 8 + 9)				

*Indicates facts well suited for using strategies based on 10 (Making 10 and Pretend-a-10)

**Indicates facts well suited for the Near Doubles strategy (although could be solved using other strategies)

TOOL 26

Progress Monitoring Tool for Multiplication Facts

	Foundational Fact Sets						Other Facts					
	× 2	× 10	× 5	× 1	× 0	Squares	× 3	× 4	× 6	× 7	× 8	× 9
Phase 1: Skip counts												
Phase 2: Uses strategy												
Phase 3: Automatic												

8

Families and Facts

Research has demonstrated a positive correlation between the level of parental involvement and a child's achievement in school (e.g., Aspiazu, Bauer, & Spillett, 1998; Henderson & Mapp, 2002). However, to maximize the benefits of their involvement, parents need information directly from school leaders and teachers about their child's mathematics program, including *how* instruction might differ from their own experiences and *why* those changes have been made. Information about fact fluency is especially important because most adults view the teaching of basic facts as "basic"—you drill or show flash cards for every fact until your child can say the correct answer quickly. Helping parents understand the fundamentals outlined in this book builds their understanding of the goals, which guides them as they help their children master the basic facts by learning strategies and developing fluency.

This chapter provides ways to work with parents to identify alternative approaches to fact practice at home and connects to the five fundamentals in these ways:

1. **Mastery must focus on fluency.** Parents and other stakeholders need to understand that, although we want every child to master the basic facts, the way to reach this goal is by focusing on fluency, not rote memorization.

2. **Fluency develops in three phases.** A major focus of this chapter is providing parents with the strategies (Phase 2), games to work on those strategies, and questions to ask to help their children progress through the phases.

3. **Foundational facts must precede derived facts.** Since we come from a tradition of learning facts in order from least to greatest and have focused primarily on counting and memorizing, it is critical to communicate the progression you are using and why it is important.

4. **Timed tests do not assess fluency.** Some people equate the use of timed tests with assessment of fluency or automaticity. You must help parents see that these are two different things and that there are many better ways to work on automaticity. Timed tests can actually work *against* that goal.

5. **Students need substantial and enjoyable practice.** Practice at home is critical but should be meaningful and stress-free through games, strategy talk, and self-assessing progress.

Your commitment to changing the culture of basic fact learning and assessment must include families. Without strong communication, your instructional plan can encounter resistance and skepticism; with communication, your plan can find support, collaboration, and success. It just makes sense that whatever is fundamental to your basic fact fluency plan be shared with families.

Changing Parental Mindsets

Because the common mindset is that basic facts are something that should be taught the way they have always been taught, you must consider ways to illuminate the errors in those practices while building confidence in a different approach. For example, sharing the five basic fact fundamentals can help parents reflect on the quality of the resources they see at the bookstore or online. For example, they may be considering an app that provides engaging ways to show flash cards with time limits to win a round. As described in Fundamental #4, such time pressures can work against their child's emerging number sense. Here we share some ways to help change mindsets and introduce parents to the full meaning of fluency.

Debunking the Myths About Fact Fluency

We begin this section with what we find to be some of the most pervasive ideas about basic fact mastery throughout the larger school community, including among parents. Some of these statements have been accepted as truths simply because basic facts have always been taught or thought about in a certain way. The first one is intended for you, the teacher; the latter ones are for sharing with families (and students). Although we call out these myths and facts here to set the tone for the chapter, we will return to them later as we offer actual activities to debunk (and hopefully correct) the myths.

Myth: *Parents want flash cards and timed tests as part of their child's basic fact learning experience.*

Fact: Parents want their children to be automatic with their basic facts (a learning outcome) more than they desire one particular instructional or assessment approach. The reason these practices might be popular with parents (or tutors) is because that is how they learned the facts; they may not be aware that other approaches exist. Educating and involving families is therefore critical. For the parent who still believes that flash cards and timed tests work, they can offer such experiences at home (although we are not recommending this).

Myth: *Memorization is the best technique to master basic facts.*

Fact: Rote memorization is not effective for learning and retention (Willis, 2006). Children may remember in the short term and then forget. Rote memorization of basic facts has the added flaw that, if you forget the fact, you have no alternatives for figuring it out efficiently. If the memorized fact is forgotten, the alternative is to count (addition) or skip count (multiplication). Neither is efficient. It is much more effective for students to apply number relationships to develop fluency, and eventual mastery, of basic math facts. Eventually, children either come to know the facts *from memory*, or they become so automatic at selecting and applying strategies that they can generate a response within a few seconds.

Myth: *Timed tests help students master the facts.*

Fact: Research says the opposite! The more students are exposed to timed tests, the worse they perform (Henry & Brown, 2008). Additionally, timed tests cause anxiety (Engle, 2002), particularly for children with high mathematical aptitude (Ramirez et al., 2013), and that can lead to lasting fear and avoidance of mathematics.

Myth: *Games are not adequate substitutes for fact drill.*

Fact: In a given amount of time, children can practice at least as many facts playing games as they do on a worksheet (often more). Games also provide the benefits of engagement, rich discussion of math concepts, instant feedback, and an opportunity for teachers to assess strategy use and progress toward mastery.

As you progress through this chapter, you will find various ways to help address the myths and communicate these key truths with families. Gatherings such as Family Math Nights or PTA meetings are great avenues for this. However, these questions could surface at any time with parents, so it is important to be prepared with the facts about the facts.

Our Messaging to Parents

Too often, changes to elementary mathematics programs raise more concerns than congratulations. This resistance may be because parents recognize the importance of mathematics and do not want their children to be guinea pigs in ways that will be detrimental to their eventual success in this subject. Alternately, it may be that the parents just believe that the laws and principles of mathematics do not change, so they see no reason why the *teaching* of mathematics should change. As you engage in basic fact advocacy, it is important to compose your messages carefully so that your well-intended messages are not misinterpreted and so that you can help parents with their own messaging to their children.

Sometimes we say things in a certain way to keep things simple and clear for parents, but we may end up introducing concerns. Some possible examples are provided in Figure 8.1.

Notice that the last topic specifically refers to calculators. Even if parents are avid users of technology, they may have concerns about their child's use of calculators prior to mastering the basic facts. Research overwhelmingly finds that children using calculators achieve at least as well as those not using calculators (Ellington, 2003; Hembree & Dessart, 1986; Ronau et al., 2011). Consider sharing one of these two activities to demonstrate how calculators can support basic fact mastery, then follow the activity with a conversation about using the calculator as a learning tool and not as a replacement for mastering basic facts.

- Repeating numbers. Type in 5 + 5 = . Continue to push the = key. (Most calculators continue to add 5 every time you push the key.) What patterns do you notice as you count by fives?
- Broken keys. Suppose the 6 and the 8 keys do not work on your calculator. Figure out another way to add or subtract these numbers using the calculator:

    6 + 5   15 − 6   35 + 28

Meaningful Interactions with Families

Calling all teachers and administrators: Numeracy is as important as literacy! In fact, there are many parallels between numeracy and literacy. Just as students might be able to sing the alphabet but not know that K is a letter and makes a special sound, being able to count does not mean that students recognize 7 as a number or the quantity that it represents. Numeracy, like literacy, is complex and involves a blend

FIGURE 8.1   Messaging for Basic Fact Fluency

Original Statement	Possible Parent Interpretation	A Stronger, Carefully Composed Statement
"We are not going to be doing timed tests this year."	"Is she saying speed doesn't matter? Are they not working on mastering facts?"	"To do a better job determining which facts each child has learned and which ones they need to work on, we are going to be using several different assessment tools."
"We aren't going to be memorizing facts. Instead, we are going to be working on strategies to learn the basic facts."	"Why aren't they just memorizing the facts? They have to have them memorized eventually, so why waste time with strategies?"	"For students to be able to say all the facts within seconds, we are going to focus on strategies. Strategies will eventually lead to automaticity, and this way your child won't forget the facts they have learned."
"We are going to take all year to work on mastering basic facts."	"All year? What about other math topics? My child already knows the facts and won't be challenged."	"Our goal is not just to master the facts this year but also to develop fluency with the facts. This extra focus on using strategies efficiently takes time but will have big payoffs for your child with higher-level math concepts, such as multidigit multiplication and fractions. For this reason, we will work on fluency all year long."
"We are going to use calculators in our mathematics learning."	"Shouldn't they have to master the facts first? Isn't the calculator the reason why students don't know the facts today?"	"We will be strategically using calculators to support fact mastery and number sense. Calculators do not replace the need to know the facts, but calculators can support mathematics learning in many ways."

of concepts and skills. Therefore, attention to early numeracy and basic fact fluency must receive reasonable attention in the major events that bring families into the school.

Kindergarten Orientation

Many studies have shown that early numeracy is critical to future academic success (Frye et al., 2013; Watts, Duncan, Siegler, & Davis-Kean, 2014). In fact, what a 5- or 6-year-old child knows about mathematics predicts not only their future mathematics achievement but also their future reading achievement (National Research Council, 2009). Therefore, it is essential to engage everyone in understanding early numeracy and how to help children look at relationships between numbers and quantify objects, rather than exclusively focusing on saying and writing the counting sequence.

As children begin working specifically on the basic facts, understanding and using properties becomes *the* big idea of numeracy. Knowing that you can decompose 13 into 10 + 3 makes the product 13 × 15 mentally manageable. This use of the distributive property is fundamental to algebra and much of mathematics, not to mention making a child more proficient in daily uses of mathematics. However, advanced thinking like this begins with first recognizing 13 as a quantity. The kindergartner who can separate 13 bears into a pile of 10 bears and a pile of 3 bears can eventually become the 4th grader who can mentally multiply 13 × 15. It is a progression of mathematical thinking that takes years to develop, and it is important to get parents on board with understanding this from the start of the journey.

Many schools invite parents for an orientation months before the first day of kindergarten. Too often, this orientation neglects math altogether or simply mentions it briefly without explaining what numeracy looks like (e.g., "We will be working on adding numbers up to 10"). Although there are many important things to do on this day, we plead for you to include math readiness, attending to numeracy, adding to or changing what parents consider helpful in getting their child ready for school. Giving numeracy the same status as early literacy means that the kindergarten orientation cannot solely focus on literacy goals and plans but *must* also attend to numeracy goals and plans.

When parents think of how to help their child with math, they think about counting, writing numerals, and memorizing facts. Imagine, however, if they understood that developing numeracy was actually a better focus for their efforts with their child. To help parents learn an effective way to support numeracy, play a quick game with them, such as Sleeping Bears or Racing Bears (see Chapter 2), illustrating how to decompose numbers and find one less or one more than a number. Imagine parents bragging about how their child can find all eight ways to decompose seven into two addends, as compared to bragging that their child can count to 200. Although counting *is* important, counting to high numbers is not necessary for any of the critical early mathematical concepts. We need to heighten the importance of supporting numeracy; for example, playing with objects so that children begin to see what 4 looks like in lots of different ways and how it relates to 3 and to 5. This discussion at a kindergarten orientation can greatly influence what parents do over the summer to help their children be "math-ready" for school.

We recognize that not all parents attend an orientation session before kindergarten, yet it should be a priority to get the numeracy message to every family. Therefore, we must employ other ways to communicate to parents how to help their child be ready and excited for kindergarten. One idea is to create game kits for Sleeping Bears by placing a five frame, five teddy bear counters (or five teddy bear cut-outs), and instructions (translated into languages represented in the school) in plastic zipper bags. These can be distributed at registration. The bag can be a "Welcome to Kindergarten" gift and a way to start school by communicating that numeracy is important, mathematics can be fun, and it is important to talk about and do mathematics together with your child.

Back-to-School Nights

Back-to-School Nights across all elementary grades, K–5, must help parents understand the importance of computational fluency, including basic fact fluency. In the youngest grades, it can focus on the critical role numeracy and number sense serve in helping students to eventually become automatic with basic facts. For the upper grades, it can include connecting basic fact fluency to fluency with larger whole numbers, fractions, and decimals. You may wish to adapt some of the suggestions in the following section on Family Math Nights to provide a brief introduction to fluency at your Back-to-School Night. Additionally, the prompts shown in Figure 8.2 can be given to parents to aid in their support of fluency. These may be posted on your class's web page, prepared on a bookmark for parents to take home with them, glued on the inside of a take-home folder, or prepared as a magnet that can go on a refrigerator.

FIGURE 8.2　Basic Questions to Support Basic Fact Fluency

Fluency Goals:
- Accuracy
- Efficiency (time and strategy choice)
- Flexibility (uses different strategies for different problems)
- Appropriate strategy use

Questions:
- How did you solve it?
- How do you know it is correct?
- Is there another way you could solve it?
- If someone didn't know the answer to _____, how would you tell them to figure it out?
- What strategy can you use to find that fact?
- How is _____ like _____ (e.g., How is 2 × 7 like 4 × 7?)? How are they different?

Family Math Nights

Family Math Nights can serve many purposes. One purpose would be to learn how to play the games described throughout this book. Another is to help parents understand the mathematical content itself. Providing opportunities for parents to learn about mathematical ideas prior to their children learning them can lead to improved relationships with parents and increased student achievement (Knapp, Jefferson, & Landers, 2013). A third goal is to develop consistency between the way math is taught in school and how it is reinforced at home. For example, helping parents to (1) appreciate the value in learning from mistakes and (2) reflect on strategies that may make sense for a given problem is not trivial, given that many parents did not engage in these practices when they learned mathematics in school.

A major goal of any elementary school Family Math Night, however, should be helping parents develop an understanding of basic fact fluency in an enjoyable way. Here we have outlined one possible sequence of activities that we have found to be helpful and engaging. Two of the suggested activities, Parent Quizzes and Myths and Facts Sorts, will then be discussed in greater detail.

1. Have parents share what fluency means to them or engage in a Myths and Facts Sort.

2. Engage parents in a Parent Quiz or show a video of a classroom where children are demonstrating fluency, such as using or sharing strategies during class discussion or game play.

3. Develop a robust definition of fluency (flexibility, accuracy, efficiency, and appropriate strategy use) and share the three phases of fact mastery.

4. Demonstrate key fluency-building activities, such as quick looks and facts games. (Salute is an author favorite for this.)

5. Close with sharing the implications of the activity for assessment (as opposed to timed testing) or revisiting the Myths and Facts Sort.

Parent Quizzes. Making the distinction between fluency and mastery/automaticity is the crux of helping parents understand and support a basic fact fluency plan. A common concern (even criticism) from parents is that schools are teaching unnecessary strategies to their children when they could just be focusing on memorizing the facts and performing the standard algorithms. Parents deserve a sound reason for learning strategies, and that reason cannot be "It is required by the state/standards/district/textbook." Parents deserve a reason that focuses on the long-term benefits for their children. For basic facts, it can be useful to have parents reflect on how they solve addition and multiplication problems. To begin, consider asking parents to solve a series of problems like the ones in the Basic Facts Quiz in Figure 8.3.

FIGURE 8.3 **Parent Quizzes**	
Basic Facts Quiz	**Beyond the Basics Quiz**
1. $5 + 7 =$ _____	1. $95 + 7 =$ _____
2. $5 \times 9 =$ _____	2. $5 \times 49 =$ _____
3. $9 + 6 =$ _____	3. $90 + 60 =$ _____
4. $6 \times 8 =$ _____	4. $8 \times 15 =$ _____
5. $7 \times 3 =$ _____	5. $35 \times 3 =$ _____

If you feel comfortable, you can set a timer, giving parents 15 seconds to find the answers for the Basic Facts Quiz. Setting a timer gives them a chance to reflect on how they feel in a timed assessment, as well as how they felt when they were children. An advantage of timing them for this activity is to be able to then play some games and ask them to compare the two experiences in terms of how they felt and how much they practiced the facts within a given time. Regardless of whether the quiz is timed or not, once parents are finished, focus the conversation on *how* they thought about each fact. They may have just known the answer, used a strategy, or perhaps counted or skip counted. You may need to model what you mean by a strategy, giving an example for one of the facts. You may wish to elicit which strategies parents used. Every time we have given a Parent Quiz, at least some parents have used strategies, such as the Making 10 strategy for the first fact. Now you have an opportunity to talk about how mastery and fluency compare. Mastery is getting an answer automatically, or within three seconds, either through recall *or highly efficient strategy application*. If they used a strategy, they knew a strategy that worked for them for that fact. Fluency precedes automaticity, for fluent children are flexible, efficient, and strategic, but they may not yet produce answers within three seconds.

The first quiz has the purpose of making the distinction between mastery and fluency—in other words, how are they different? Next, you may wish to follow the discussion of the Basic Facts Quiz by having parents complete the Beyond the Basics Quiz. The problems in this quiz are strategically designed to show why we should care about fluency (and not just mastery) and why the time devoted to strategy instruction is a worthwhile investment. The following process can be used to address why fluency is important:

1. Invite parents to solve the Beyond the Basics problems in any way they choose.
2. Talk about any or all of them and how they solved the problem(s). Listen for several different strategies for each.
3. Explicitly point out the connections between related problems in the two quizzes, helping parents to recognize how fact strategies transfer to greater numbers. For example, if they used the Making 10 strategy for the first Basic Facts problem, they can use it to solve the first Beyond the Basics problem. Similarly, if they noticed they could take half of 6 in 6 × 8 and then double the number (3 × 8 = 24; 24 × 2 = 48), they can use that same idea for finding 8 × 15 (4 × 15 = 60; 8 × 15 = 120).

4. Summarize by noting that, although fluency requires more time and more focus on strategy instruction, it is the beginning of being able to solve more complex problems efficiently and flexibly throughout mathematics. In other words, fluency is *essential* for mathematical proficiency. It is truly a long-term investment with substantial payoffs.

Close by reminding the parents about the questions shown in Figure 8.2 or provide opportunities for them to offer ideas as to how they can emphasize this type of reasoning with their children.

Sorting truths and myths. Given the pervasiveness of myths regarding facts instruction and assessment that were discussed at the beginning of this chapter, we suggest several activities that are designed to address myths head-on and are ideal for a group setting. One engaging way to help parents begin to distinguish fact from fiction is a Myths and Facts Sort. Share a list of truths and myths early in the event (without identifying them as either truths or myths). A possible list is provided in Figure 8.4. Invite parents to sort the statements as either myths or facts. Proceed with the main content of the Family Math Night, building their understanding of fact fluency. At the end of the evening, return to the lists and elicit suggestions for reclassifying any of their original selections. Close by sharing which are myths, which are facts, and why.

A second idea for debunking myths is an activity called Two Truths and a Myth. This is an adaptation of Two Truths and a Lie, a community-building or icebreaking activity (your parent night could even begin this way so that parents in your class can learn about the other parents in their child's classroom). For the basic facts activity, provide three statements from Figure 8.4 (or ones you have created yourself) and have parents talk about which one is the myth and why.

At orientations, Back-to-School Nights, and Family Math Nights, you have a great opportunity to build support (or to instill fear!) in your approach to basic facts. Activities like the ones provided here establish a sound rationale that will resonate with parents so that questions and concerns can be addressed in an interactive way.

Math at Home

Explicitly teaching parents *how to* help their children makes a difference in increasing student achievement and improving student attitudes (Cooper, 2007; Else-Quest, Hyde, & Hejmadi, 2008; Patall, Cooper, & Robinson, 2008). At a Back-to-School Night, PTA meeting, or Family Math Night, you may wish to ask families to make a math promise (Legnard & Austin, 2014). A math promise is an explicit agreement that the family will do math together *and* get to know each other's mathematical reasoning. Family members make this promise to one another (parent to child and child to parent). Playing math games and noticing mathematics in their daily lives are two ways for doing just that.

FIGURE 8.4 **Truths and Myths About Mastering Basic Facts**	
Children eventually need to be automatic with their facts, coming up with an answer in about three seconds.	Truth
The order in which the basic facts are learned matters.	Truth
Basic fact fluency is an essential skill for performing operations with fractions.	Truth
Calculators can support students in learning basic facts.	Truth
Automaticity is the same thing as mastery.	Truth
Memorization is the best technique to master the basic facts.	Myth
Timed tests help students master the facts.	Myth
Games are not adequate substitutes for fact drill.	Myth

Games

Unlike workbooks, games provide opportunities for mathematical discussion. For example, asking "How did you solve it?" and "What reasoning strategy might you use?" helps students to develop and practice strategies and parents to hear those strategies. This encourages parents to focus on fluency and not just automaticity. Instead of always assigning traditional homework, occasionally send home specific games (this book offers more than 40 options) as homework. Provide instructions that ask parents to play the game several times with their child and encourage the child to write a summary of what happened as they played. (They can note a strategy they used frequently, a fact they "mastered," or a pattern they noticed.) Younger children can dictate as their parents write their summaries. Any of the games in this book are appropriate for playing at home. The key is to play them first at school so the student understands how to play the game.

Math in Daily Life

Math reasoning is a part of many daily tasks, and using a "think aloud" can help children turn these daily tasks into meaningful math practice. Teach parents to practice the #noticewonder protocol, asking their child to look at something that might be mathematically interesting and asking, "What do you notice?" Then, after brainstorming some noticings, ask, "What do you wonder?" Curiosity is so critical to learning and loving mathematics, and this practice helps students to see how math can be used to answer real life questions (curiosities). Beyond the endless opportunities for notice and wonder conversations, parents can ask questions that target their child's mathematical learning. Your task is to help parents learn to put on their "mathematical lenses" at home and in the car. During a PTA meeting, Family Math Night, or Back-to-School Night, you can offer the ideas here as a start and have the parents brainstorm other ideas for math talk in their daily lives.

- As socks are folded, ask, "How many socks did we wash?" [doubles] and "How did you figure that out?" [counting, skip counting, grouping]
- At dinner, there may be 12 dinner rolls (or other food that will be shared). Ask, "How might we share these rolls?"
- As bedtime or time to leave is approaching, ask, "How many more minutes until _____?"
- For chores or household tasks, ask how long it will take to [clean each bathroom, bake all the cookies, plant all the flowers] if there are x number of [bathrooms, batches of cookies, flowers to plant].
- Talk about today's date. Ask the child to look at the date and think of different addition (or multiplication) facts that have that number as the solution; also, ask what else they know about that number. For example, if it is the 12th of the month, the child might think that $10 + 2 = 12$ or $3 \times 4 = 12$, and they may relate 12 to the number of eggs in a carton or a number on a clock (Mistretta, 2013).
- In the car, ask, "Do you see a basic fact on that license plate?" or "Can you add the numbers on that license plate?"

- In the car, select a target number, such as 20 for younger children or 100 for older ones. Ask the child to use the numbers on a license plate to reach that target number (Hildebrandt, Biglan, & Budd, 2013). For example, given the number 60, an older child might multiply two 8s to make 64 and then subtract four to reach the target number of 60.

Finally, magazines, catalogs, newspapers, television, and the internet frequently offer opportunities to think about math. Invite parents to try to notice just one thing in the upcoming week, and that will help them to see that there are math talk opportunities everywhere.

Supporting Accurate Communication Between Parent and Child

A final and essential component of communicating basic fact fluency is helping parents with *their* messaging. We sometimes hear parents say, "I am not good at math" or "I don't like solving math problems," often as a reason for why their child is struggling. However, we know there is no math gene! When parents say things like this to their children, it can impede their child's success in mathematics. In fact, a parent's emotions are connected to the student's emotions, and a positive attitude about school has been connected to better academic performance (Else-Quest et al., 2008). It is our responsibility as educators to point this out to families and help them to portray mathematics in a positive light. For example, rather than saying, "I never learned my multiplication facts," they might instead say, "The 8s facts were hard for me, too, so I decided to use the strategy of finding the 4s fact and doubling it." Small changes in a parent's messaging can lead to big changes in their child's confidence, perseverance, and disposition.

Conclusion

All the suggestions for developing and assessing fluency that you have encountered throughout this book depend on students having the confidence to take risks and attempt reasoning strategies when learning basic facts. We have focused on five fundamentals of developing fluency that we believe are important for all teachers, parents, administrators, and other stakeholders to understand to ensure *every* child develops basic fact fluency and is thereby prepared to become mathematically proficient. We have worked with countless students over many years and have seen first-hand the difference a focus on fluency can make in their learning and retention of facts, as well as in their confidence and mathematical identities. Focusing on strategies, playing strategy games, and using interviews and self-reflection leads to students who are confident and competent in solving problems. Some may call these problems basic, but we know that they are the foundation from which much more mathematics emerges. It is our sincere hope that the tools provided in this resource, along with other resources you create, will help you implement a basic fact plan that leads to every student reaching fluency and lasting fact mastery.

References

Aspiazu, G. G., Bauer, S. C., & Spillett, M. D. (1998). Improving the academic performance of Hispanic youth: A community education model. *Bilingual Research Journal, 22*(2), 1–20. doi: 10.1080/15235882.1998.10162719

Baroody, A. J. (1995). The role of the number-after rule in the invention of computational shortcuts. *Cognition and Instruction, 13*(2), 189–219.

Baroody, A. J. (2006). Why children have difficulties mastering the basic number combinations and how to help them. *Teaching Children Mathematics, 13*(1), 22–31.

Baroody, A. J., Bajwa, N. P., & Eiland, M. (2009). Why can't Johnny remember the basic facts? *Developmental Disabilities Research Reviews, 15*(1), 69–79.

Baroody, A. J., Purpura, D. J., Eiland, M. D., Reid, E. E., & Paliwal, V. (2016). Does fostering reasoning strategies for relatively difficult basic combinations promote transfer by K–3 students? *Journal of Educational Psychology, 108*(4), 576–591.

Bay-Williams, J. M., & Kling, G. (2014). Enriching addition and subtraction fact mastery through games. *Teaching Children Mathematics, 21*(4), 238–247.

Bay-Williams, J. M., & Kling, G. (2015). Developing fact fluency: Turn off timers, turn up formative assessments. In C. Suurtamm (Ed.), *Annual perspectives on mathematics education.* Reston, VA: NCTM.

Bay-Williams, J. M., & Stokes Levine, A. (2017). The role of concepts and procedures in developing fluency. In D. Spangler & J. Wanko (Eds.), *Enhancing professional practice with research behind principles to actions.* Reston, VA: NCTM.

Boaler, J. (2012). Timed tests and the development of math anxiety. *Education Week.* Retrieved from https://www.edweek.org/ew/articles/2012/07/03/36boaler.h31.html

Boaler, J. (2014). Research suggests that timed tests cause math anxiety. *Teaching Children Mathematics, 20*(8), 469–474.

Brendefur, J., Strother, S., Thiede, K., & Appleton, S. (2015). Developing multiplication fact fluency. *Advances in Social Sciences Research Journal, 2*(8), 142–154. doi: 10.14738/assrj.28.1396

Caldwell, J. H., Kobett, B., & Karp, K. (2014). *Putting essential understanding of addition and subtraction into practice, pre-K–2.* Reston, VA: NCTM.

Carpenter, T. P., Ansell, E., Franke, M. L., Fennema, E., & Weisbeck, L. (1993). Models of problem solving: A study of kindergarten children's problem-solving processes. *Journal for Research in Mathematics Education, 24*(5), 428–441.

Carpenter, T. P., Fennema, E., Franke, M. L., Levi, L., & Empson, S. (2014). *Children's mathematics: Cognitively guided instruction* (2nd ed.). Portsmouth, NH: Heinemann.

Clements, D. (1999). Subitizing: What is it? Why teach it? *Teaching Children Mathematics, 5*(7), 400–405.

Cooper, H. (2007). *The battle over homework: Common ground for administrators, teachers, and parents* (3rd ed.). Thousand Oaks, CA: Corwin.

Council of Chief State School Officers & National Governors Association. (2010). *Common core standards for mathematics.* Retrieved from http://www.corestandards.org/wp-content/uploads/Math_Standards1.pdf

Dennis, M. S., Sorrells, A. M., & Falcomata, T. S. (2016). Effects of two interventions on solving basic fact problems by second graders with mathematics learning disabilities. *Learning Disabilities Quarterly, 39*(2), 95–112.

Ellington, A. J. (2003). A meta-analysis of the effects of calculators on students' achievement and attitude levels in precollege mathematics classes. *Journal for Research in Mathematics Education, 34*(5), 433–463.

Else-Quest, N. M., Hyde, J. S., & Hejmadi, A. (2008). Mother and child emotions during mathematics homework. *Mathematical Thinking and Learning, 10*(1), 5–35. doi: 10.1080/10986060701818644

Engle, R. W. (2002). Working memory capacity as executive attention. *Current Directions in Psychological Science, 11*(1), 19–23.

Frye, D., Baroody, A. J., Burchinal, M., Carver, S. M., Jordan, N. C., & McDowell, J. (2013). *Teaching math to young children: A practice guide* (NCEE 2014–4005). Washington, DC: National Center for Education Evaluation and Regional Assistance, Institute of Education Sciences, U.S. Department of Education. Retrieved from https://ies.ed.gov/ncee/wwc/PracticeGuide/18

Fuson, K., & Kwon, Y. (1992). Korean children's single-digit addition and subtraction: Numbers structured by ten. *Journal for Research in Mathematics Education 23*(2), 148–165.

Gersten, R., Beckmann, S., Clarke, B., Foegen, A., Marsh, L., Star, J. R., & Witzel, B. (2009). *Assisting students struggling with mathematics: Response to Intervention (RtI) for elementary and middle schools* (NCEE 2009-4060). Washington, DC: U.S. Department of Education, Institute of Education Sciences, National Center for Education Evaluation and Regional Assistance. Retrieved from https://ies.ed.gov/ncee/wwc/PracticeGuide/2

Gersten, R., & Clarke, B. S. (2007). *Effective strategies for teaching students with difficulties in mathematics* (NCTM Research Brief). Retrieved from https://www.nctm.org/Research-and-Advocacy/Research-Brief-and-Clips/Effective-Strategies-for-Teaching-Students-with-Difficulties

Godfrey, C. J., & Stone, J. (2013). Mastering fact fluency: Are they game? *Teaching Children Mathematics, 20*(2), 96–101.

Heege, H. T. (1985). The acquisition of basic multiplication skills. *Educational Studies in Mathematics, 16*(4), 375–388.

Hembree, R., & Dessart, D. J. (1986). Effects of hand-held calculators in precollege mathematics education: A meta-analysis. *Journal for Research in Mathematics Education, 17*(2), 83–99.

Henderson, A. T., & Mapp, K. L. (2002). *A new wave of evidence: The impact of school, family, and community connections on student achievement.* Austin, TX: Southwest Education Development Laboratory.

Henry, V. J., & Brown, R. S. (2008). First-grade basic facts: An investigation into teaching and learning of an accelerated, high-demand memorization standard. *Journal for Research in Mathematics Education, 39*(2), 153–183.

Hiebert, J., & Carpenter, T. P. (1992). Learning and teaching with understanding. In D. A. Grouws (Ed.), *Handbook of research on mathematics teaching and learning* (pp. 65–97). New York: Macmillan.

Hiebert, J., & Lefevre, P. (1986). Conceptual and procedural knowledge in mathematics: An introductory analysis. In J. Hiebert (Ed.), *Conceptual and procedural knowledge: The case of mathematics* (pp. 1–27). Hillsdale, NJ: Lawrence Erlbaum Associates.

Hildebrandt, M. E., Biglan, B., & Budd, L. (2013). Let's take a road trip. *Teaching Children Mathematics, 19*(9), 548–553.

Jordan, N. C., Kaplan, D., Locuniak, M. N, & Ramineni, C. (2007). Predicting first-grade math achievement from developmental number sense trajectories. *Learning Disabilities Research and Practice, 22*(1), 36–46.

Jordan, N. C., Kaplan, D., Nabors Olah, L., & Locuniak, M. N. (2006). Number sense growth in kindergarten: A longitudinal investigation of children at risk for mathematics difficulties. *Child Development, 77*(1), 153–175.

Jordan, N. C., Kaplan, D., Ramineni, C., & Locuniak, M. N. (2009). Early math matters: Kindergarten number competence and later mathematics outcomes. *Developmental Psychology, 45*(3), 850–867. doi: 10.1037/a0014939

Kamii, C., & Anderson, C. (2003). Multiplication games: How we made and used them. *Teaching Children Mathematics, 10*(3), 135–141.

Kling, G., & Bay-Williams, J. M. (2014). Assessing basic fact fluency. *Teaching Children Mathematics, 20*(8), 488–497.

Kling, G., & Bay-Williams, J. M. (2015). Three steps to mastering multiplication facts. *Teaching Children Mathematics, 21*(9), 548–559.

Knapp, A. K., Jefferson, V M., & Landers, R. (2013). Learning together. *Teaching Children Mathematics, 19*(7), 432–439.

Kouba, V. L. (1989). Children's solution strategies for equivalent set multiplication and division word problems. *Journal for Research in Mathematics Education, 20*(2), 147–158.

Legnard, D., & Austin, S. (2014). The math promise: Celebrating at home and school. *Teaching Children Mathematics, 21*(3), 178–184. doi: 10.5951/teacchilmath.21.3.0178

Locuniak, M. N., & Jordan, N. C. (2008). Using kindergarten number sense to predict calculation fluency in second grade. *Journal of Learning Disabilities, 41*(5), 451–459.

Mistretta, R. M. (2013). "We do care," say parents. *Teaching Children Mathematics, 19*(9), 572–580.

Montague, M. (1997). Cognitive strategy instruction in mathematics for students with learning disabilities. *Journal of Learning Disabilities, 30*(2), 164–177.

Mulligan, J. T., & Mitchelmore, M. C. (1997). Young children's intuitive models of multiplication and division. *Journal for Research in Mathematics Education, 28*(3), 309–330.

Myers, A. C., & Thornton, C. A. (1977). The learning disabled child learning the basic facts. *Arithmetic Teacher, 25*(3), 46–50.

National Research Council. (2001). *Adding it up: Helping children learn mathematics.* J. Kilpatrick, J. Swafford, & B. Findell (Eds.). Mathematics Learning Study Committee, Center for Education, Division of Behavioral and Social Sciences and Education. Washington, DC: National Academies Press.

National Research Council. (2009). *Mathematics learning in early childhood: Paths toward excellence and equity.* Washington, DC: National Academies Press.

Patall, E. A., Cooper, H., & Robinson, J. C. (2008). Parent involvement in homework: A research synthesis. *Review of Educational Research, 78*(4), 1039–1101.

Purpura, D. J., Baroody, A. J., Eiland, M. D., & Reid, E. E. (2016). Fostering first graders' reasoning strategies with basic sums: The value of guided instruction. *The Elementary School Journal, 117*(1), 72–100.

Ramirez, G., Gunderson, E. A., Levine, S. C., & Beilock, S. L. (2013). Math anxiety, working memory, and math achievement in early elementary school. *Journal of Cognition and Development, 14*(2), 187–202. doi: 10.1080/15248372.2012.664593

Ronau, R. N., Rakes, C. R., Rush, S. B., Driskell, S., Niess, M. L., & Pugalee, D. (2011). Using calculators for teaching and learning mathematics. Technology Research Brief series. Retrieved from https://www.nctm.org/uploadedFiles/Research_and_Advocacy/research_brief_and_clips/2011-Research_brief_18-calculator.pdf

Schoenfeld, A. H. (1991). On mathematics as sense-making: An informal attack on the unfortunate divorce of formal and informal mathematics. In J. F. Voss, D. N. Perkins, & J. W. Segal (Eds.), *Informal reasoning and education* (pp. 311–343). Hillsdale, NJ: Lawrence Erlbaum Associates.

Swanson, H. L. (1990). Instruction derived from the strategy deficit model: Overview of principles and procedures. In T. Scruggs & B. Y. L. Wong (Eds.), *Intervention research in learning disabilities* (pp. 34–65). New York: Springer-Verlag.

Thornton, C. (1978). Emphasizing thinking strategies in basic fact instruction. *Journal for Research in Mathematics Education, 9*(3), 214–227.

Thornton, C. (1990). Subtraction strategies: Subtraction number facts. *Educational Studies in Mathematics, 21*(3), 241–263.

Tournaki, N. (2003). The differential effects of teaching addition through strategy instruction versus drill and practice to students with and without learning disabilities. *Journal of Learning Disabilities, 36*(5), 449–458. doi: 10.1177/00222194030360050601

Van de Walle, J. A., Karp, K. S., & Bay-Williams, J. M. (2019). *Elementary and middle school mathematics: Teaching developmentally* (10th ed.). New York: Pearson.

Vasilyeva, M., Laski, E. V., & Shen, C. (2015). Computational fluency and strategy choice predict individual and cross-national differences in complex arithmetic. *Developmental Psychology, 51*(10), 1489–1500. doi: 10.1037/dev0000045

Verschaffel, L., Greer, B., & De Corte, E. (2000). *Making sense of word problems.* Lisse, the Netherlands: Swets & Zeitlinger.

Watanabe, T. (2003). Teaching multiplication: An analysis of elementary school mathematics teachers' manuals from Japan and the United States. *The Elementary School Journal, 104*(2), 111–125.

Watts, T. W., Duncan, G. J., Siegler, R. S., & Davis-Kean, P. E. (2014). What's past is prologue: Relations between early mathematics knowledge and high school achievement. *Educational Researcher, 43*(7), 352–360. doi: 10.3102/0013189X14553660

Wheatley, G. H., & Reynolds, A. M. (1999). *Coming to know number: A mathematics activity resource for elementary teachers.* Bethany Beach, DE: Mathematical Learning.

Willis, J. (2006). *Research-based strategies to ignite student learning.* Alexandria, VA: ASCD.

Index

About the Authors

 Jennifer M. Bay-Williams, PhD, is a mathematics teacher educator at the University of Louisville, Kentucky. She has written many articles and books related to K–12 mathematics education, including the popular *Elementary and Middle School Mathematics: Teaching Developmentally* and the related three-book series, *Teaching Student-Centered Mathematics*. Other recent books include *Everything You Need for Mathematics Coaching*, *On the Money* (financial literacy), and *Developing Essential Understanding of Addition and Subtraction*. Bay-Williams is a national leader in mathematics education, having served as a member of the National Council of Teachers of Mathematics (NCTM) Board of Directors, secretary and president of the Association of Mathematics Teacher Educators (AMTE), lead writer for the *Standards for Preparing Teachers of Mathematics* (AMTE, 2017), and a member of the TODOS: Mathematics for ALL Board of Directors. Bay-Williams taught elementary, middle, and high school students in Missouri and in Peru. She currently works in elementary classrooms in the Louisville area, helping teachers and students attain basic fact fluency while also developing strong mathematical identities. Follow Bay-Williams on Twitter (@JBayWilliams) or contact her directly at j.baywilliams@louisville.edu.

 Gina Kling is fortunate to serve the mathematics education community in a variety of ways. Since 2011, she has worked as a curriculum developer for the elementary mathematics curriculum *Everyday Mathematics* (based at the University of Chicago) with a focus on grades K–3. Recently she served as the grade 1 lead author for the *Everyday Mathematics 4 State Editions*, the author of the *Everyday Mathematics 4*

Quick Looks Activity Book, and one of the authors of *Everyday Mathematics for Parents: What You Need to Know to Help Your Child Succeed*. Kling has taught mathematics content and methods courses for the past 15 years at Western Michigan University in Kalamazoo, Michigan, and is also currently completing a doctoral degree in K–12 mathematics education at Western Michigan University. For more than a decade, Kling has focused her research on helping children learn basic math facts in meaningful ways and often shares her work through professional development with practicing teachers across the country. She has authored numerous articles on teaching and assessing basic facts and remains active in the elementary classroom today as a mathematics coach, engaging children in developing fact fluency. Kling can be contacted directly at gina.garza-kling@wmich.edu.

Related ASCD Resources

At the time of publication, the following resources were available (ASCD stock numbers in parentheses).

Books

Building a Math-Positive Culture: How to Support Great Math Teaching in Your School (ASCD Arias) by Cathy L. Seeley (#SF116068)

Lesson Imaging in Math and Science: Anticipating Student Ideas and Questions for Deeper STEM Learning by Michelle Stephan, David Pugalee, Julie Cline, and Chris Cline (#117008)

Making Sense of Math: How to Help Every Student Become a Mathematical Thinker and Problem Solver (ASCD Arias) by Cathy L. Seeley (#SF116067)

The School Leader's Guide to Building and Sustaining Math Success by Marian Small and Doug Duff (#118039)

Teaching Students to Communicate Mathematically by Laney Sammons (#118005)

Unpacking Fractions: Classroom-Tested Strategies to Build Students' Mathematical Understanding by Monica Neagoy (#115071)

Quick Reference Guides

Games and Tools for Teaching Addition Facts (Quick Reference Guide) by Jennifer Bay-Williams and Gina Kling (#QRG118020)

Games and Tools for Teaching Multiplication Facts (Quick Reference Guide) by Gina Kling and Jennifer Bay-Williams (#QRG119016)

Guiding Meaningful Math Conversations (Quick Reference Guide) by Laney Sammons (#QRG117056)

For up-to-date information about ASCD resources, go to **www.ascd.org.** You can search the complete archives of *Educational Leadership* at **www.ascd.org/el.**

ASCD myTeachSource®

Download resources from a professional learning platform with hundreds of research-based best practices and tools for your classroom at http://myteachsource. ascd.org/

For more information, send an e-mail to member@ascd.org; call 1-800-933-2723 or 703-578-9600; send a fax to 703-575-5400; or write to Information Services, ASCD, 1703 N. Beauregard St., Alexandria, VA 22311-1714 USA.

THE WHOLE CHILD

The ASCD Whole Child approach is an effort to transition from a focus on narrowly defined academic achievement to one that promotes the long-term development and success of all children. Through this approach, ASCD supports educators, families, community members, and policymakers as they move from a vision about educating the whole child to sustainable, collaborative actions.

Math Fact Fluency relates to the ***engaged*** and ***challenged*** tenets. *For more about the ASCD Whole Child approach, visit* ***www.ascd.org/wholechild.***

WHOLE CHILD **TENETS**

1 HEALTHY
Each student enters school healthy and learns about and practices a healthy lifestyle.

2 SAFE
Each student learns in an environment that is physically and emotionally safe for students and adults.

3 ENGAGED
Each student is actively engaged in learning and is connected to the school and broader community.

4 SUPPORTED
Each student has access to personalized learning and is supported by qualified, caring adults.

5 CHALLENGED
Each student is challenged academically and prepared for success in college or further study and for employment and participation in a global environment.